Plain Selling

CGW
PUBLISHING

2017

Plain Selling

First Edition: January 2017

ISBN 978-0-9565358-5-6

Published by:

CGW Publishing
B 1502
PO Box 15113
Birmingham
B2 2NJ
United Kingdom

www.cgwpublishing.com

mail@cgwpublishing.com

genius

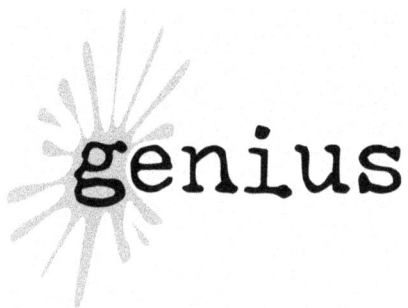

www.geniuslearning.co.uk

peter@geniuslearning.co.uk

Contents

Exercises

1:   Welcome

Learning is an investment in the future.

It's an investment in you, and it's an investment in your business.

Without learning, you would have to figure everything out by trial and error, and when other people have figured things out for you, it's wise to benefit from their knowledge.

Knowledge defines our culture. The rise of technologies such as the printing press, the television, mobile phones, the internet and social media demonstrate how much we like and need to acquire and share knowledge. Our survival depends on knowledge.

Learning isn't an accident, though. It's an organised, predictable process, and if you understand how it works, you can use it more effectively.

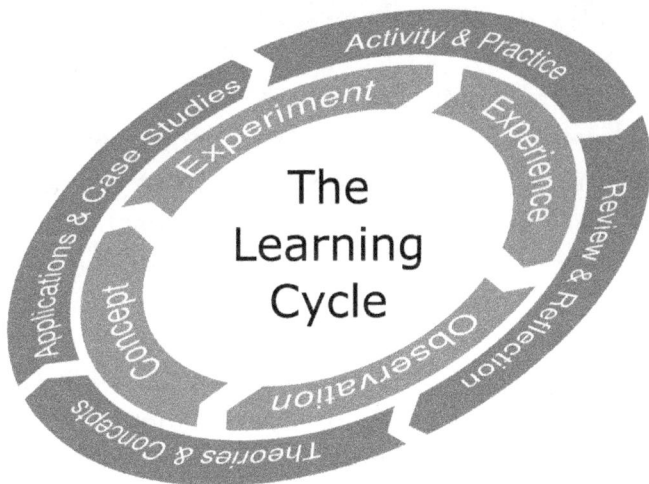

The
Learning
Cycle

Activity & Practice
Experience
Review & Reflection
Observation
Theories & Concepts
Concept
Applications & Case Studies
Experiment

Learning is at its most effective when you can combine the activities of the learning cycle so that you learn something new, try it out for yourself, discover how and why it works and make it your own. Your brain is wired up for learning, both through your own experiences and by observing others, and it is an incredibly efficient machine, able to reinforce useful connections and delete ones which are no longer serving you.

People often say, "practice makes perfect", however, this isn't strictly true. It's more accurate to say, "practice makes permanent". So practice isn't in itself important, what you must do is practice the right things.

Probably the single biggest problem in corporate training today, particularly in the areas of sales and management (or 'leadership' as it may mistakenly be called) is that people who are experience sales professionals or managers think they're good trainers. They think that, because they were good at something, they will be good at teaching other people to do it.

If you've experienced sales training then I'm sure you've seen the self-assured 'been there, done it' trainer whose essential message is, "I was awesome, so do what I do and you'll be awesome." Unfortunately that doesn't work. Firstly, because it's extremely unlikely that he or she was, indeed, awesome. Hence they're not selling any more. Secondly, because as good as they were, they were good in their world, with their products, with their customers, and the world has changed since then. We could say that the profession of sales is changing at a faster rate now than ever before, with the adoption of technology into the sales process. Finally, and most importantly, they know how to *be* good sales people, but they have forgotten how to *learn* to be good sales people. That's what a sales trainer needs to be good at. Not doing, but learning to do.

In this book, which you can think of as a workshop in itself, I'm not going to say much about technology, for the simple reason that the people who say that technology enables sales are of course the people selling the technology. In my view, which you may or may not agree with, technology is a barrier to sales, because technology prevents people from having direct, personal, individual relationships. Using CRM and 'big data' to personalise your junk emails is not a relationship. Creating an interactive app to streamline the customer acquisition process is not a relationship. Picking up the phone or, better, going to meet people at events and interest groups – that's the start of a relationship.

In this workshop, we are going to work together to discover what are the 'right things' for you. We're going to share experiences and discuss best practice. We're going to try out new ideas and new skills. And we're going to share feedback so that we can discover what works.

Learning is never a passive activity, so you can't learn a skill just by listening to someone else describe it. You have to join in, take part, share your own ideas and make mistakes. Because by sharing what we all know, we can create something new, together.

2:   What is Sales?

Sales is... well, what do you think it is?

2.1   Sales

What does 'selling' mean?

What is the purpose of selling?

How does a customer see a salesperson?

For our purposes, let's assume the following:

What does 'selling' mean?

Selling is the management of a new customer's interaction with your business.

What is the purpose of selling?

Its purpose is to manage that interaction in a controlled way so that you can predict and therefore influence the customer's transaction.

How does a customer see a salesperson?

As a barrier? As someone who will make me buy something I don't want? As a gatekeeper? 20 years ago, the salesperson was the customer's source of market knowledge, now that place has been taken by Google. The salesperson is therefore someone who understands how to negotiate the complex ordering process and make life easy for the customer. The salesperson might also have knowledge which adds value to that process, but the salesperson first has to earn the right to apply that knowledge.

Let's say that sales is an organised approach to guiding a potential customer through a decision process which ends with that customer paying money for, and receiving, a product or service.

There are two sides to sales:

- Strategy, which is what you do before you talk to a customer

- Tactics, which is what you do when you're talking to a customer

Easy!

What you have to do is make sure you're doing the right things at the right times. Some sales people stick rigidly to the 'sales cycle', others say that they're a creative, dynamic, responsive sales virtuoso who likes to be flexible. In other words, they have no plan and are working reactively, which means the customer is calling the shots, which means they'll never be in control of the deal. The best sales people I've ever met are also the most organised, methodical, analytical people I've ever met.

And by 'best', of course I mean sales results. After all, your job as a sales person is to secure new business. In some big companies, sales targets are very complicated, with metrics for customer satisfaction, customer retention, product types, service delivery and so on. However, none of these things pay the bills today. In any business, it's important to balance short term income with long term growth, so any good sales person will always deliver business that is good today and for the future.

If you just want to know the secret to being a great sales person then here it is: make sure you're doing the right things at the right times. I know I've already said that, but that really is all there is to it. The trick is to know what the right thing is, and to figure out when the right time is.

The answers are in this book, of course.

3:   Excellent Salespeople

What are the qualities of a great salesperson?

They might include:

- Energetic
- Likeable
- Enthusiastic
- Confident
- Intelligent
- Tenacious

- Knowledgeable
- Good communicators
- Persuasive
- Influential
- Credible
- Friendly
- ?

In fact, probably the most important quality of a great salesperson is that they are **organised**.

Everything else on that list is nice, but ultimately irrelevant. We all buy from salespeople who we don't like, who are dull and disengaged, because we don't actually care about the salesperson, we only care about getting our hands on the thing we want.

3.1   Your Greatest Asset

> As a salesperson, what is your single most valuable asset?

I've modelled the very best sales people in all kinds of industries, which means that I have analysed their perceptions, thought processes and behaviours to figure out how they do what they do. The result is always that the very best sales people see their most valuable asset as their own time. Their respect for their own time makes them focus on what they can win and it gives the appearance of them respecting the customer's time too. So that's good all round.

Your business has a business plan, including a set of goals and some ideas for how you're going to achieve those goals. But in between those future goals and your present reality is a gap, and that gap is going to be filled by sales people. The job of a sales manager is to make sure that they do that as efficiently as possible, getting the job done with the least amount of time and effort, because when the sales team works efficiently, it can achieve more with the resources available. Fewer people can sell more. The team can work on fewer, bigger deals. And you can move faster, because remember that in business, it's not the big that eat the small, it's the fast that eat the slow. As Charles Darwin pointed out, the species that are most successful are the ones most able to adapt to change, and in the global recession, we have seen time after time that the companies that survive and grow aren't the biggest or best, they're the ones that could react and adapt most quickly, turning a threat into an opportunity to change and thrive.

For the past 14 years, I have been working with sales leaders and sales teams, and the most common problem that I find, the most common reason that sales teams don't perform as well as they could, is that the behaviour of sales people is not aligned with the business plan, and that is absolutely the job of the sales manager.

Most companies engage sales training to change sales peoples' behaviour, however I have found that behaviour is almost never the problem; it's one of measurement and focus.

3.2   Behaviour and Results

Probably the majority of sales managers, particularly when results aren't as good as they should be, focus on managing behaviour. Whilst these sales managers would never like to admit it, their underlying belief is, "I would have closed that deal if it had been mine. If these people just do what I tell them to do, everything will work properly." It's an illusion of control; if I could control everything then the world would be a better place.

Examples of a focus on behaviour are:

1. Make 20 sales calls per day

2. Send out 30 brochures per week

3. Follow the sales script

4. Tell the customer three benefits

5. Leave the customer with a product sample

When you focus on behaviour, it's almost impossible to fire an under-performer. When you focus on results, it's more black and white; they get the result or they don't. How close someone needs to get to the result is for you to decide, because that is all about the standards that you personally maintain. However, if you set goals and allow your staff to consistently fail to reach them, you send the message that performance is optional.

The downsides of the controlling manager's belief are that it puts a great deal of pressure on the sales manager to be perfect, and it means that sales people aren't responsible for results:

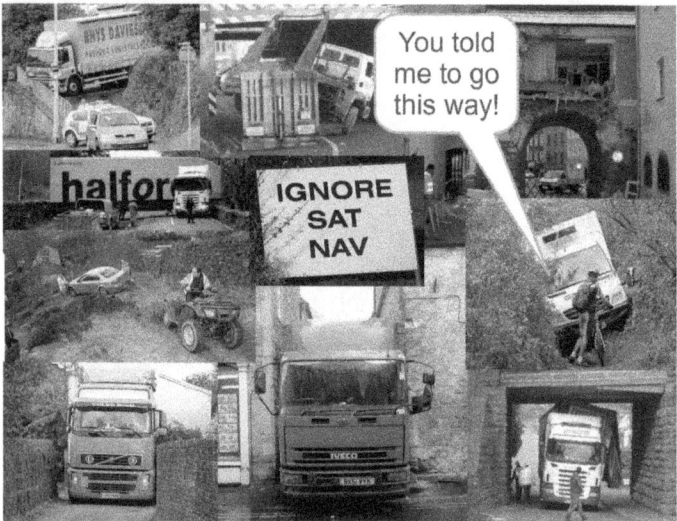

The alternative to this is a focus on results. When you hold people accountable for achieving results, you also have to give them some freedom in how they achieve those results.

Examples of a focus on results include:

- Deliver £5m in new order revenue

- Create 10 new partner relationships

- 50% of revenue from new customers

However, you need to decide what you want those results to cost you. Let's say that yourself hit your sales target, but with an enormous expenses bill. If your expenses don't come out of your salary, why should you care? At the extreme, you might think that you don't care what happens to the rest of the business as long as you're on target.

The senior managers at a large defence engineering business thought this way, and they ended up throwing more and more contractors at the problem of poor project management, where the cost of under-performance was at least £16 Million per year, including contractor costs and penalty payments which meant that the company would have made more profit if it hadn't won any contracts.

The managers of a leading specialist retailer I've worked with focus on results, with the consequence that their store managers run their stores how they like and get paid far more than store managers in other retailers. Everyone is so busy chasing results that there is little consistency in how those results are delivered, and the business strategy changes from one month to the next as the MD gets impatient that the latest strategy isn't working quickly enough.

Focusing on results has its downside too:

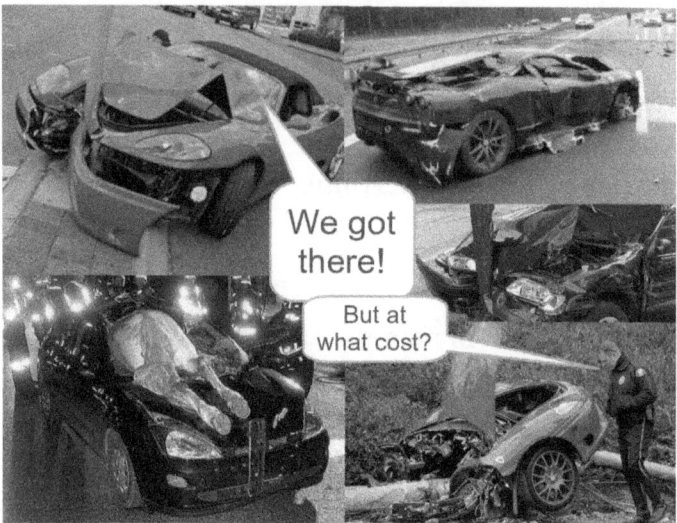

3.3   The Best Sales People

The best sales people are very efficient time managers. They are focused and committed. And they do absolutely the minimum to get paid the maximum. Sales people really define a business, because they are the human face of it. They are the first people to speak to customers, and they create the first impression and set the customer's expectations. It doesn't matter what your product or service is, your customers will learn about it from the way you behave in those early sales interactions.

If you are on time, honest, reliable and helpful, the customer will automatically assume that this is way that everyone in your business will behave. They will expect your products to be reliable. They will expect your website to be honest. They will expect your customer service to be helpful. The customer learns everything about your company from their first interaction with you.

And if you not sure about a product, or you say something just to get the customer to place an order, or if you forget to mention some anticipated problems with delivery, or if you don't send information when you promise to, your customer will automatically assume that your products and services will be unreliable, that they can't trust what anyone says, that they can't count on you.

When a customer buys from you, they are not buying because they think you are nice, or because your product looks interesting, or because they have nothing better to do. They are buying from you because they expect you to add value to their business. They expect you to solve a real problem that costs them real money. They expect you to help them respond to new opportunities. They expect you to do what you say you will do. They expect to be able to count on you.

I said that the best sales people are very efficient, and actually some people would say that they are lazy. But this is quite normal and it's a good thing, because it means that they really understand their business very well. They are hired to do a very simple job, and paid when they do that job well. So the very best sales people learn how to do that job as well as they can, and with the least effort possible. Sales people are very important in a business because, every day, they are testing the market and getting real feedback from customers. But that doesn't mean that they should decide on product or pricing strategy. Anyone can give a product away, but only an expert can create real value.

The first and most important secret of the best salespeople is that they know that their single most valuable asset is their own time. All of these secrets actually arise from this first one.

Valuing their own time makes them qualify hard. In fact, they're almost ruthless. When they first speak to a potential customer, they find out if they're talking to the decision maker, what the budget is, who the competitors are and so on. Yes, we all know that we should ask those questions, but it's often easier not to because it's uncomfortable to ask a question when you don't want to know the answer. But why would a sales person not want to know about the customer's budget? Because if the customer says that they don't have a budget, the sales person has to find someone else to talk to. If they don't ask, they can be busy without having to worry about being productive. They can send out brochures and go to meetings and never have to worry about their results. The best sales people only worry about their results.

The second secret is that they take personal responsibility for what they do and the results they get.

The very best sales people don't blame their competitors or products when they lose a sale – they know that there is only one reason to lose, because they didn't do enough to win it. This responsibility makes them connect their behaviour with their results. They don't rely on chance and luck, they rely on their own knowledge and skills.

The third secret is that they focus their time and effort on what they can control.

They don't fool themselves into thinking that they can control the customer's decision, but they do know that they can ask questions, solve problems and anticipate objections so that they can control as many variables as possible. They try to take all of the uncertainty out of the sales cycle, or as much as they can. If they know they're not going to win a deal, or they can see that a competitor clearly has a better solution, they qualify out, walk away and spend their valuable time doing something that will bring them real results.

The fourth secret is that they prioritise based on hard, rational business criteria.

Average sales people prioritise based on what's easy or comfortable, or what they like doing, or what makes them feel good. They put off unpleasant tasks, where the best sales people treat every job the same. Why? Because they know that every job, from making cold calls to taking a customer out to lunch is just one step in a much bigger journey. When the best sales people prioritise, they're always consistent. They don't sit at their desks, wondering what to do today. They already know.

The fifth secret is that they value the customer relationship over the sale.

If they can't deliver the right solution for the customer, they say so. They don't waste their own time, or their customer's trying to make the wrong solution fit. They are honest, saying, "we can't help you this time, but I'd like to keep talking to you about projects that we're better suited to". They tell the customer the truth, and that makes the customer trust them more. They don't look for a 'quick win' that will only make the customer unhappy, they would rather walk away this time and win better and bigger business next time.

The sixth and final secret is that they always sell what the customer needs, not what they want.

Rather than take the easy option and just give the customer what they ask for, they ask tough, deep questions. They challenge the customer. They even tell the customer that they're wrong. They build trust and credibility, and when the customer asks for their advice, they give it, honestly and directly. They know that if the customer's ego gets in the way, then the deal wasn't fair or right anyway. They challenge the customer to think deeper about their needs and address real business problems, and that makes the customer do a better job for their business. By challenging the customer's needs, they help the customer to become stronger.

3.4   Summary

- Time is their most important asset

- Take responsibility for their results

- Focus on what they can control

- A relationship is more important than a sale

- Prioritise tasks based on logic not emotion

- Work hard to uncover the real needs

3.5   Goals

We all have goals; some goals are explicit, we know what they are and we consciously work towards them, such as, "I want to get home on time today". Other goals are implicit, they guide our behaviour but we don't necessarily think about them, such as, "I want to feel like I've achieved something".

What is your outcome or goal as a salesperson?

Your implicit goals shape your behaviour. They define how you answer the telephone, how you talk to a customer, what questions you ask, and what you do when the customer says, "I'll think about it."

Having clear outcomes, expressed in a certain way, actually makes it easier for you to achieve them. The following process is a way of refining your goals so that you can focus your time and energy on achieving them.

3.6   Taming the Sales Monster

Ask your friends to describe a salesperson and they will probably say things like chatty, personable and results oriented. Ask people who aren't worried about hurting your feelings and they might say pushy, arrogant and flashy.

The biggest hurdle that you will ever have to get over in order to master sales is not tough customers, nor aggressive competitors, nor challenging market conditions. First, you have to tame the sales monster that lives inside you.

You had an experience of sales long before you got involved in sales for a living. You had experiences of being sold to, and you heard horror stories from other people about being sold to, ripped off, conned, stitched up and so on. You heard from friends and relatives about dodgy cars, decrepit houses and all manner of things which did not live up to the stunning expectations created by the sales person. In fact, 'salesperson' became synonymous with 'untrustworthy'. Who would want to talk to, or spend money with, someone like that? If your mental image of a salesperson is of a pointy-haired, pointy-shoed, sharp-suited, fake-tanned smooth talker, or a big-haired, pointy-shoed, short-skirted, fake-tanned smooth talker, then you will spend your working life trying to prove that you are not that person. The more you try to prove it, the more you become that person, because that is your point of reference. Try as hard as you can not to be a sausage. Go on. I dare you. Try really hard. You see? The harder you try not to be a sausage, the more you realise that you are, in fact, a sausage.

Your secret preconception of the worst type of salesperson is your own personal sales monster.

Monsters are entities that we never see or hear, yet we know they're real, because otherwise our fears would be irrational. We create monsters in order to explain why we avoid certain things, and make excuses for things we haven't done.

It's natural to fear rejection. It's natural to internalise a memory of someone else being rejected. We're a social species and our survival depends on acceptance. When we see someone being rejected, we quickly learn not to do what they did for fear of the same result. That's how we build monsters in our minds.

For you to be a naturally, easily, effective salesperson, you have to tame that monster, and the way to do that is to acknowledge its existence, and then to laugh in its face.

First, picture the person who you would hate to be seen as by your customers or friends. That's the monster. Then ask yourself, seriously, what is it that you are most afraid of, that the monster represents? Don't say 'nothing' because that's not normal. You're afraid of rejection, of not being liked, of not being good enough, of failure, of success, of being judged, of not being perfect, of being lost. You need approval, respect, trust, love. You need to be liked and cared for. And as a salesperson, you've thrown yourself into the job where you're most likely to have those fears provoked by rejection and the threat of failure, which will make you act out of insecurity and desperation.

All is not lost. When you acknowledge those fears, you own them, and when you own them, they can have no power over you.

Whenever you find yourself putting more energy into something than seems reasonable, or you find yourself putting something off that you really should get done, you are being motivated by fear. Acknowledge it, and then make a choice about your next action.

I know it's a cliché to say either do something or don't do it, however it really is true. Instead of having some sales actions sitting on your 'to do' list for weeks, acknowledge the fear that's keeping them there and either tackle them or discard them, do one or the other. It's your choice, no one is forcing you either way.

Fundamentally, remember that you'll only ever lose a deal through lack of information, and your only barrier to being all that you want is yourself. The solution to both of those is simply to ask more questions.

3.7   An Outcome for Learning

1 What do you want from this workshop?

2 How will you know when you have it?

3 What will having it do for you?

4 What will having it do for your customers?

5 What do you need in order to get it?

6 What can the people around you do to help you get this?

7 What stops you from achieving this now?

8 What can you see yourself doing differently as a result of this workshop?

4:   Types of Sales

Most peoples' experience of sales comes from being on the receiving end of consumer or B2C sales. When a business sells to another business, that's called B2B sales.

4.1   Defining Sales Terms

Can you fill in the blanks? I've suggested some answers at the end of the book.

Type	Who is the customer?	Who is the salesperson?	What's the risk?
Direct			
Indirect			

Channel	Reseller	Retail	Wholesale	Outsource
			Wholesale buyer	
			Manufacturer or importer	
			No control over sales to user	

4.2   Direct and Indirect

We have an added layer of complexity when we consider a chain of sales relationships. We generally only think in terms of a salesperson selling to a user, however this is almost never the case. Most of the time, a number of transactions take place in a sequence called a 'supply chain'.

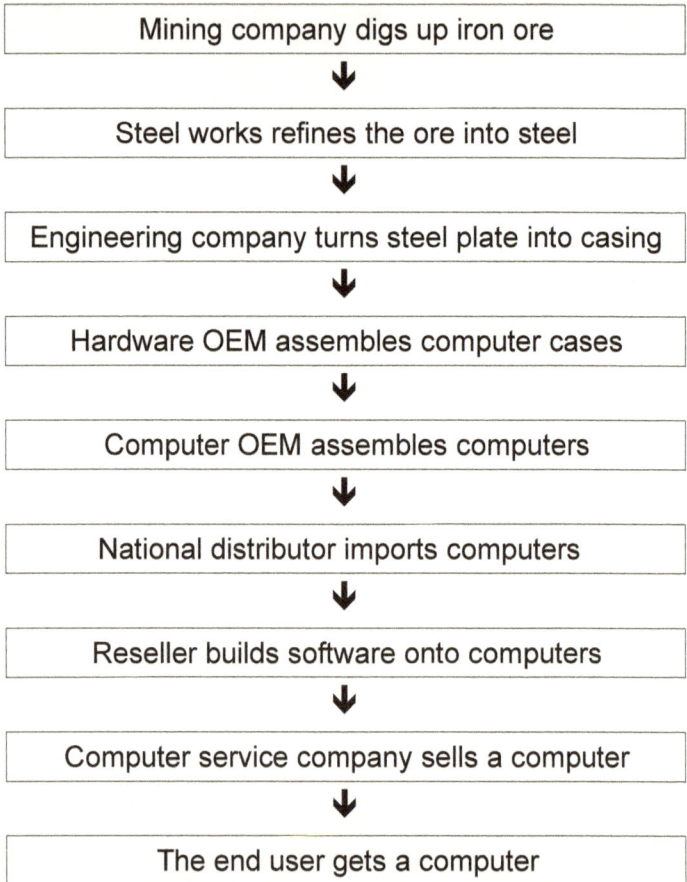

Mining company digs up iron ore

↓

Steel works refines the ore into steel

↓

Engineering company turns steel plate into casing

↓

Hardware OEM assembles computer cases

↓

Computer OEM assembles computers

↓

National distributor imports computers

↓

Reseller builds software onto computers

↓

Computer service company sells a computer

↓

The end user gets a computer

We haven't even looked at the supply chain involving the user of the computer yet! Each of these links needs sales people and buyers to manage the sequence of processes.

Direct selling is generally regarded as selling to the end user, and indirect is where we're selling to someone who then sells to an end user. In reality, the transactions within a business don't form a neat 'supply chain' because many different products and services come together to serve many different customers.

If you own a grocery shop, is the person who comes in to buy a bag of flour the end user? Or is it the person they're baking the birthday cake for? Or is it the guests at the birthday party?

Some companies have two types of salespeople, one team sells to a corporate buyer, the other tries to influence the end user. This is known as 'pull-through' selling or 'demand creation'.

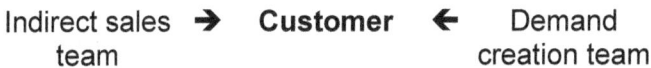

| Indirect sales team | ➜ | **Customer** | ← | Demand creation team |

In this instance, the customer is typically a buyer in a reseller company, such as a retailer or wholesaler. Sales people go and pitch to the buyers, and of course the buyers could choose from many similar products to serve their own customers. By creating demand, the demand creation sales team gives the buyer an incentive to select their products, because the buyer knows that customers will already be interested.

Usually, the job of demand creation is done through general marketing and advertising. The difference with a demand creation sales team is that they will speak to a specific customer about buying specific products, and then allow that customer to choose the best reseller to get those products from. With marketing, you can't really see who is looking at your adverts and leaflets, and you don't know which of your competitors they're also looking at.

The answer to the question of who is the end user or customer in your grocery shop is easy to understand when you think about what a bag of flour actually is. It is a bag of flour. A bag, containing flour. That's it.

Therefore, the person who comes in to buy it is the end user, because when they get home and bake the birthday cake, the flour is no longer flour, it is now a cake. The end user is the person who consumes the product or service. Anyone else, such as the guests at the birthday party, is a **stakeholder**. Not a direct decision maker, but perhaps an **influencer**.

4.3 Inbound and Outbound

We also have to consider the direction of the sales relationship. This usually refers to the first contact with a potential customer, so if you're calling them, that's an outbound call, and if they're calling you, that's an inbound call. You need to handle them differently.

Direction	Who made the first call?	Why?	What does the customer want?	What's the outcome for the call?
Outbound				
Inbound				

The important point to remember here is that when the customer calls you, they are not having their first experience with your company. They are calling because they have seen or read something, or spoken to someone, and they therefore have expectations. They are calling because they believe you can help them.

4.4　Direct and Indirect

With direct selling, the person who buys the product or service is the person who will use it for its primary purpose.

With indirect selling, the person who buys the product or service is doing so because of its added value, not because of its primary purpose.

Imagine you have a small engineering company.

A classic car enthusiast might buy a part from you to restore a car. He is the customer, the buyer, the decision maker and the user.

A maintenance company might buy a part from you to repair a customer's machine. The end user doesn't know who supplied the part. The added value is that the part you supply enables your customer to repair something for their customer.

A company that stocks parts for classic cars might order a batch of a particular part from you so that they can supply their customers, who might be either car owners or car parts retailers. The added value is that they have the part in stock, so it's available immediately for customers.

Therefore the real value of a product or service is the cost plus the value to the customer, and each customer will perceive value differently.

The larger the customer's business, the more likely they are to have professional buyers who manage supplier relationships to deliver best value, which generally means getting the best product and the best service at the best price.

The important point to take from this is that you need to know who you are selling to, because the person who you're talking to might be a decision maker, end user or recommender, or all three.

4.5   Who is the Customer?

Contact:	Decision Maker	End User	Recommender
Example:			

5:   Products and Services

Are products and services the same? Do we sell them in the same way?

No. Definitely not. They are fundamentally different.

Let's first define what a service actually is:

"A service is an activity which adds value to a product"

Here are a few examples.

Product	Service
Carpet	Fitting
Medical consumables	Application
Computers	Set-up
Books	Delivery

I know. It's ridiculously simple.

What do we mean by "adds value"? Simply, that the service allows you to charge more for the product, and therefore makes it more valuable for the customer because it saves them the time and cost and hassle of having to do something themselves. You could fit your own carpets and car tyres, or install your own computer software, or go and fetch your own books from the shop, but it's easier to pay someone else to do it.

When salespeople talk about "adding value", they really just mean, "charging more money". However, the customer won't simply pay more money for the same product, they expect something in return, and that's added value.

Often, the cost of these types of services is hidden within the price of the product. We're so used to getting free delivery or fitting that most people wouldn't consider paying for the service, even if the overall cost was less.

Unless you are manufacturing something yourself which is in high demand relative to its supply, your margins on product sales will be low. Some retailers operate on a margin of around 1%. Computer distributors might get closer to 4%.

You can see that, in a pure product sales business, you have to keep operating costs extremely low, and that often means that you end up cutting corners, which impacts on the customer's perception of your products.

Some products are difficult to use without an element of service. Unless you're a trained carpet fitter or computer technician, you need someone else to make the product usable for you. Hence, what often see in a retailer's advertising is:

Product	Service
Carpet	Free fitting
Computers	Free set-up
Books	Free next day delivery

If you have a carer or visiting nurse who comes to your home to check how your operation is healing up, he or she might apply new dressings, and that is a service that you might not perform yourself.

We know that, in reality, those services are not free, we know that we pay a higher price for books and carpets in order to have them delivered and fitted. We have to take those costs into account when calculating our margins and hence our sales costs.

We could say that every business delivers an element of service, in that an activity has to take place to get the product to the customer. Many companies train their staff to deliver good customer service, however there is a big problem with this...

You can not provide good customer service

Good service is what the customer **experiences**

As we'll see in a while, trying to deliver good customer service can actually have a negative impact on your turnover.

There are many companies which focus more on services, or even completely on services.

An engineering company might offer design consultancy, installation and support, the value of which far outweighs that of the products sold.

A training or consultancy business might offer only services, with no tangible products changing hands. However, we can count knowledge, or Intellectual Property, as a product in this case, because IP can be recorded in physical form, and it can be protected.

We intuitively know that we like to visit shops that treat us well, however you can probably also think of instances where you've received outstanding service from a shop, restaurant or hotel, and you have never been back, perhaps because of its location or some other factor. You can perhaps also think of places where the service is just average, yet you go there regularly.

Service can be a differentiator, but if your customer doesn't know that they're getting something special, they are unlikely to notice. All that you actually achieve is to reset their expectations at a higher level, so now you have to work even harder to keep them happy.

Retailers such as Amazon and ebay create a problem in the market. With next day, or even same day delivery, instant refunds, no-quibble returns and so on, these retailers don't just skew the customer's expectations for their own businesses, they affect what a customer expects from all businesses. When a corporate buyer gets next day delivery and an instant refund from Amazon for one book, he expects the same service when he's buying a multi-million pound computer network for his employer, too.

As a salesperson either selling a service, or using service as a differentiator, your biggest problem is that you think that good service increases profits, and that's not the case.

Research from the Association for Consumer Research on "Market Orientation and Customer Service" found a very strong connection between five links in the chain of events that connect service to profit:

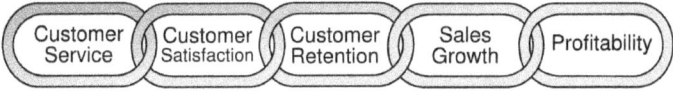

| Customer Service | Customer Satisfaction | Customer Retention | Sales Growth | Profitability |

However, other studies have found no significant connection between service and profit!

The answer to this might be found in another research study from the University of Maryland, entitled, "Linkages between customer service, customer satisfaction and performance in the airline industry"

This research found that the connection between service and profit is 'non-linear', in other words, it's not a simple, direct connection, where more customer service = more profit.

Quality of Customer Service (x-axis)

Profit (y-axis)

Better service leads to increased profits up to a certain point, and then it doesn't matter how much better your service is, your profits decline because the customer doesn't care and that extra service costs money.

5.1 The Service Chain

To increase your profits through service, you have to understand how your own service chain links together, and in order to do that, you have to be able to measure activities.

How can you measure performance in each of the five links in the service chain? Identify a measure and a suggestion for improvement for each.

Customer service

Customer satisfaction

Customer retention

Sales growth

Profitability

Here's a simple example.

Customer service How many carpets do we fit each week?
Customer satisfaction How many customers leave positive reviews?
Customer retention How many customer return or recommend?
Sales growth How much do those customers spend?
Profitability What profit is achieved from that customer spend?

The fundamental key to success in sales is **measurement**. If you can't measure it, then you can't track its impact on your turnover. If you're an employed salesperson on a guaranteed bonus in a big company, who cares? If you're self-employed then reducing your costs by removing non-essential activities is quite important, mostly because that then enables you to spend your time on activities which *do* increase your income.

Research in 2013 from the Miller Heiman Research Institute found that companies that measured customer-focused behaviours had an average increase in profitability of 13% compared with other companies. This performance gap increased to 25% when combined with measurements of best practices in selling and sales management.

Examples of the customer-focused behaviours measured include:

- We use a formal process for measuring customer satisfaction and loyalty

- Our salespeople have a solid understanding of our customers' business needs

- We clearly understand our customers' issues before we propose a solution

- We have relationships at the highest levels with all our most important accounts

- In an average week, our sales force spends sufficient time with customers

Let's put these three findings together.

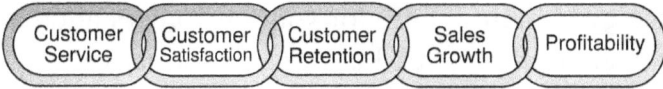

| Customer Service | Customer Satisfaction | Customer Retention | Sales Growth | Profitability |

Profit (y-axis)

Quality of Customer Service (x-axis)

Measuring customer service behaviour	› 13% increase in profit
Measuring customer service and sales behaviour	› 25% increase in profit

It's very important to note that this is relative to the customer's expectations of service. The 'optimum service level' depends on the company's brand image which in turn creates those customer expectations. Clearly, Harrods' customers expect something different than Carrefour's customers, but the same trade-off applies to both; once that optimum level is achieved, doing more for your customers adds no value, and may even be counter-productive.

This connection between expectation and delivery could perhaps be summed up with:

Your customers are happiest when you do what you say you're going to do

Why is there a connection between measuring activity and improving results?

Perhaps because, when you measure people doing the right things, they tend to do more of those things, because once they know they're being measured, they want to excel.

Measuring activity also allows you to **give feedback at the right time.**

What happens when you measure activity and give recognition for the right behaviours?

Come up with some ideas for how you can make use of these three pieces of research.

Customer Service → Customer Satisfaction → Customer Retention → Sales Growth → Profitability

Profit

Quality of Customer Service

Service behaviour → 13%
Service and sales behaviour → 25%

5.2   The Balance of Risk

In any sales transaction, there is a balance of risk which shifts from one side to the other. Both the seller and the buyer are happy when the risk is evenly shared between both parties.

Product and service sales differ most in this shifting balance of risk.

When you sell a physical product, the risk is that the customer won't be happy with it, for whatever reason. They take a risk that they end up with a product which isn't right for them, and you end up with their money and won't give it back. Consumer laws protect the buyer in such cases, and give the buyer confidence to take the risk to buy your product. With any mass produced product, the buyer can see an example so that they know what to expect.

You can therefore choose a carpet, or a fitted kitchen, or a new car based on your experience of the sample in the showroom. If you're not happy with the specific item that you receive, you return it and get a refund.

With a service, the seller cannot of course take the service back. You cannot unfit a carpet or untrain a group of managers. With a service, time only flows in one direction.

With a product sale, the risks balance out *before* the customer commits their hard earned cash, because they know that they can return the product and get a refund.

With a service sale, the risks balance out *after* the customer makes that commitment, which makes the salesperson's job more complicated. The customer has to be absolutely certain that they're going to receive exactly what they hoped for.

You can therefore expect that, where a service has been applied to a product, such as fitting a carpet, you won't be able to return it because you don't like it, but only in the case of a fault such as damage to the carpet caused during either manufacture or fitting.

Of course, *every* product sale includes some element of a service, because consumer laws require consumer protection through warranties and returns.

The more that a service element makes up the package you're selling, the more risk there is on the buyer, because they don't really know what the service will be like until they've received it, and then it's too late to give it back for a refund.

Imagine you go to a restaurant. The descriptions in the menu sound great, but what the waiter delivers is way below your expectations. What do you do? In a worst-case scenario, you leave without paying and the restaurant loses a little bit of money from the ingredients but a lot more potential income from the time that you spent at the table, preventing another customer from sitting there.

Highly commoditised 'fast food' outlets, which I can't bring myself to call 'restaurants', solve the problem by providing the exact same food, everywhere in the world, with handy pictures on the menu to show you what to expect.

Of course, there is still a margin of error, and you might still end up with something other than what you expected.

Here's a photo from such a menu:

And this is what I actually found in the box:

By the time I got home, I couldn't be bothered to go back and complain. I also didn't have any confidence that a replacement would be any better, and there we have the essence of the problem with service sales – confidence, also known as credibility.

What does credibility mean? It's the quality derived from the word credo, meaning 'I believe'. Confidence is the quality derived from the word confide, meaning to 'have trust'. Credibility and confidence both mean that the buyer believes that they will get what they expect from you.

With product sales, you don't need much credibility as a salesperson, because the product is what it is, the customer can look at it and fiddle with it, and if they don't like it they can give it back. They don't have to like you, and they don't have to trust you. In the language of Jim Holden's model, you can be at level 1 and if the product is good, you'll do OK.

With service sales, your credibility is everything. If the customer doesn't trust and believe you, they will project that lack of confidence onto the service. It doesn't matter how many years of experience your engineers have between them, or how many accreditations your service desk has, or what your testimonials say, if the customer doesn't believe you, it's game over.

Building trust is the subject of endless books and articles from business gurus who advocate team building exercises, coaching your customers, showing integrity, finding win-win outcomes, making eye contact and using an up-to-date social media profile photo.

All nonsense, of course. Trust is automatic. All you have to do to maintain it is do what you say you're going to do. Whether that's sending an email, calling when you say you will, sending the information that you promised, anything. What you do creates the buyer's expectation of what your service will do.

6:   The Sales Cycle

Why do we say that sales is a cycle rather than a process?

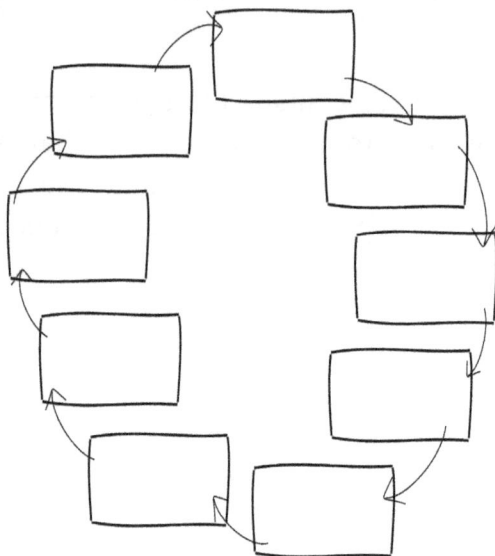

Because we want our customers' repeat business. It's much cheaper to acquire than new business, and it stops your competitors from gaining an advantage in your market. Every order that a customer places with you is a new sales lead.

In the 1980s, Jim Holden developed a new approach to selling, and in the book that went with it (Power Base Selling), he defined four types or levels of salesperson.

	Focuses on...	Behaviour	Prospects
1	Not being rejected	Happy if a customer engages in a conversation	New
2	Closing the sale	Qualifies hard and pushes to close the deal	New
3	Generating repeat sales	Gets to know the buying process	Existing
4	Building a relationship	Gets to know the customer and their business	Existing

Sales people operating at levels 1 and 2 tend to focus on new leads and don't revisit existing customers. Sales people operating at levels 3 and 4 tend to focus on 'farming' existing customers and sometimes shy away from generating new prospects. So other than level 1, it isn't a case of which approach is best, it's a case of matching the sales approach to the customer.

For example a corporate buyer for a large systems integrator will have many potential requirements and a level 3 salesperson is a good match; understanding the procurement process, getting to know the influencers, using the customer's language etc.

However, a smaller company where you're dealing with an end user is more likely to be a good match for a level 2 salesperson who pushes for the order and then moves on to the next lead. A level 2 salesperson might be pushy, they might be very tactful and patient. Their personality and their working environment don't change their focus on winning an order.

Even a level 1 salesperson will still win orders, but he or she is unlikely to be in control of the conversation, and their sales performance will be unpredictable. The main reason that we measure so much in sales is that we try to predict what our sales performance is going to be.

It's easy to think that we just want salespeople to sell as much as possible, and this is a mistake that small businesses often make. What we really want is for salespeople to sell exactly as much as we want them to so that we can plan our other business resources accordingly.

If we give salespeople uncapped bonuses, the best ones will figure out the quickest way to sell over their targets to earn as much money as possible. They might then create problems with delivery, because you don't have enough stock, or enough installation engineers, or enough money in the bank to buy the stock and pay the engineers.

Cashflow is a very important issue for any business. Whatever you do for a living, you understand cashflow. You know that you can't go to the pub until after payday. You could probably buy a new carpet, on credit, which means you would pay more for it in the long run.

Let's assume that you close a massive deal today for some computer hardware, a project which will take 6 months to implement. The customer signs the contract but won't pay anything until after they have accepted the completion of the project. In order to implement the project, your company has to buy the computer equipment and pay the people who will install it. Meanwhile, you have been paid your handsome bonus and are sunning it up in some all inclusive resort in the Caribbean. Half way through the project, your company runs out of cash and ceases to exist.

There are several problems with this. Your company should have:

- Set your target to act as a disincentive to winning such a big project

- Not paid your bonus until the project was completed, giving you an incentive to manage the customer relationship

- Negotiated a staged payments plan with the customer to cover the up-front costs

- Negotiated longer payment terms with the computer hardware manufacturer

That's all well and good in hindsight. I'm sure you'll find yourself another good sales job anyway. After all, everyone wants to hire a salesperson who smashes their targets.

Usually, sales people don't have to worry about things like this. It's someone else's problem to set their target and bonus system correctly and manage the resources of the business.

Once salespeople start thinking about the wider business impact of their activities, they move up those Holden levels.

6.1   The Buying Process

When anyone makes a buying decision, they
follow a consistent process:

Information	Decision	Buying	Owning
Finding out about what is available, potential suppliers	Narrowing down choices, making a decision	Buying the product, asking about credit, delivery, warranty etc.	Taking receipt of the product and using it

The problem with this is that when a customer
calls to place an order, they are in 'buying mode'.
They have already diagnosed their own problem,
found the solution and now they are just looking
for a supplier who can deliver it quickly at the
lowest price. When a customer is in buying
mode, there is hardly any room for you to
differentiate your service and you can only
compete on speed and price.

Asking questions means that you can understand
how the customer arrived at their decision, and
you can understand the information that was
available to them.

As for the image of a salesperson as someone who likes to tell the customer how much he or she knows about the product, the market or what is best for the customer, here's another old saying...

The customer doesn't care how much you know until they know how much you care

Listening to the customer, understanding their needs and making sure that you know as much background as possible will ensure that what you deliver isn't just what the customer asked for, it's much more than that.

Ultimately, delivering what the customer asked for is the most basic service that you can provide. The customer will be satisfied, but probably won't think twice about it.

Getting referrals and recommendations isn't about providing a great product, it's about the service that you wrap around that. Understanding the customer, anticipating their needs and helping them to solve their problems is what will delight a customer and give them a reason to recommend you to others, or to act as a reference for case studies.

6.2 Decisions

The sales cycle is a sequence of decisions. Later on, we'll start to measure what's happening at each of these decision points. For now, we need to understand exactly what happens during each of these decisions, and what that means for the role of the salesperson.

In order for you to make a decision about anything, you need these three things:

- Information

- Outcome

- Need

So that's like a decisION then.

Think about something you bought recently. You needed Information, about what was available, you had a Need to solve a problem and you had an Outcome in mind, so you imagined that your purchase would solve your problem.

Sometimes your problem is more tangible, such as running out of milk or facing a huge repair bill for your car, and sometimes your problem is more conceptual, such as the problem created by advertising which makes you think you need something only because you don't already have it.

Earlier, I talked about the balance of risk, and actually this takes place at every decision point.

You buy milk on the way home because you have run out of milk (Need) and you want to have a nice cup of tea this evening (Outcome). You pass a shop (Information) so you stop to buy milk. At this point you are balancing the risk of the milk not meeting your expectations with the cost, so you check the 'best before' date before paying for the milk, because the most likely risk is that the milk will be off, or is 'short dated' so that it will be off before you finish using it. The risk will be that you think you can have milk on your cereal, but you can't because it's gone off.

If your lifestyle means that milk frequently goes off before you've finished using it, you might mitigate the risk by buying long life milk and keeping a stock in your kitchen cupboard.

Every decision you make edges you closer to a purchase. Do you want milk? Do you have milk?

Do you have time to buy milk? Will you pass a shop on the way home that sells milk? Will the shop have milk in stock? Will the milk be within its 'best before' date? Will you have enough money?

You're not aware of this sequence of decisions, yet they influence your behaviour. With a bigger purchase such as a car or house, or your decision to change jobs, you're much more aware of the decision points and the risks that have to balance out at each decision point in order for you to move forwards.

This reveals an absolutely critical point about sales in general – that at any point in the decision process, your objective is **not** to sell, it is only to move the customer to the next decision point.

No matter how hard I try to sell you milk, or a new car, or a house, if you don't currently need one, you won't buy it. That doesn't mean that you'll never buy those things from me, it just means that you won't buy them *now*.

Sales 'experts' and trainers generally simplify this, saying that the customer or prospect doesn't have a need. That's not true. You do have a need for milk, a car and a house, but if those needs are currently met then you won't make a decision to move on in the buying process. However, you might make a decision, right now, to make a note of the new convenience store that's opened around the corner, or the car you saw yesterday that you like the look of, or the new housing development by the river that might be worth a look in the future.

Sales targets make salespeople artificially focus on what they can win before their next bonus, but this usually comes at the expense of developing a pipeline of future business.

When you think in terms of moving your prospects to the next decision point, you're no longer focusing only on the prospects who are ready to place an order.

I'm sure you have a friend who you only hear from when they want something. You might also know someone who is only nice to you when they want something. How do you feel about them? That's how we feel about salespeople who only call when we've got money to spend.

When you're supporting your prospect through the series of decision points, you're only focusing on moving to the next decision point. So when you're just starting to think about a new car, a salesperson rambling on about financing or their fantastic extended warranty is irrelevant, and will quite likely put you off, because you're not at the point where you can consider such things.

I'm sure you've experienced such a pushy 'hard sell', and it feels pushy because the salesperson is trying to jump ahead of where you are in your decision process. No matter how much I ask a bag of flour if it's ready to place an order yet, it still takes over 3 hours for my breadmaker to produce bread.

There are ways that some salespeople and retailers try to push the prospect ahead of their decision process. They might include anything from time-limited discount offers to outright threats, such as, "Today is the last day of this opportunity, if you think about it overnight then tomorrow will be too late, you have to go ahead now!" Yeah, right, I'm sure you will still be happy to take my money tomorrow.

While we've seen the concept of the 'sales cycle' to show the general stages that the sales process will progress through, in fact what we really have is a much more intricate series of decisions which either lead to a purchase or not. At every stage, the ultimate decision is to continue or not, and that's a decision as much for you as it is for your prospect. After all, you don't have to do business with everyone you meet.

7:   Sales Data

Good sales people are organised, methodical and their decisions about what to do are driven by sales data. Most of all, they know that their most valuable asset is their own time.

In turn, sales data is part of the information required to run a business. Understanding sales data is critical in managing a business, because sales data represents all of the income that a business earns in order to pay its employees and suppliers. A business exists to sell products and services, and the reality of life is that customers don't turn up on your doorstep with their cheque books in their hands; you have to go and find them. It's therefore very important to know which activities lead to sales so that you can focus your efforts for maximum returns.

You'll also need to know when to expect that income. An employee knows when it's pay-day and plans accordingly for important purchases such as takeaway pizza and beer. Thus, the last Friday of the month is generally the busiest in the pubs and bars of your local town centre.

By understanding how much it costs to make a profit, you know how to work out the minimum that you can sell a product or service for.

Profit = Sales revenue − Fixed costs − Variable costs

What your customers pay

Rent
Council tax
Employed staff
Depreciation
Internet

Cost of sale
Raw materials
Waste
Contract staff
Electricity
Telephone
Transport

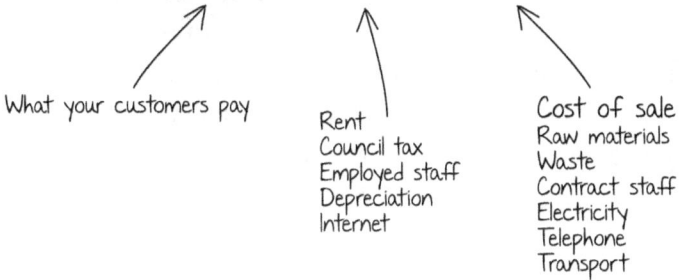

Simple! Costs for different things work in different ways, though.

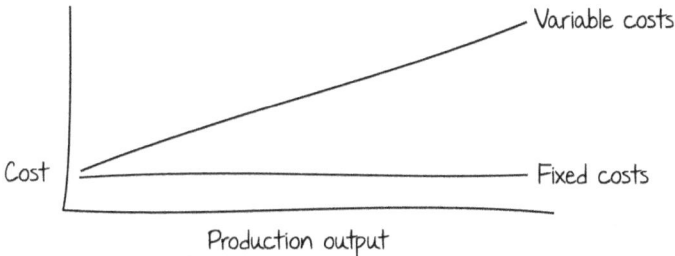

Cost

Variable costs

Fixed costs

Production output

There are some 'fixed costs' which don't change with usage or demand, so we have to make sure that our total sales income will be high enough to cover those to begin with. Therefore, we have to be confident that we're going to sell enough to cover those fixed costs. Then we have 'variable costs'. These increase as we sell or produce more, so we have to make sure that our sales margin on each sale covers those costs.

I often see business owners, usually small business owners, hiring sales people and telling them to just sell as much as they can, because lots of sales is good. Actually, lots of sales is not good. Predictable sales is good. Predictable sales let you know when to expect pay-day.

One of the most important measurements in sales is your **conversion ratio**.

At each stage of the process, you will reduce the number of customers that you are dealing with. You could say that each stage of the sales cycle serves to focus your time and effort onto the people most likely to buy from you.

If you send out 1,000 prospecting emails and receive 10 replies then your conversion rate at that stage is 1%. By identifying the points in your sales cycle at which potential customers make decisions, and by calculating the conversion ratios at each point, you can target your time and effort, thereby increasing your conversion rates. Because higher conversion rates lead to either more orders or fewer prospects, your cost of sale reduces and your profits increase.

Sales people often talk about a 'pipeline' or 'funnel':

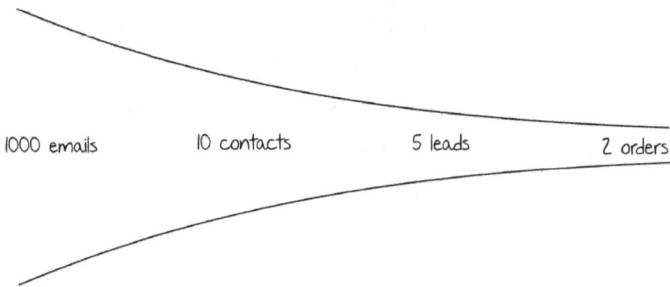

1000 emails   10 contacts   5 leads   2 orders

When you know your conversion ratios, you can calculate how many prospects will generate the income needed for the business, and you can target your lead generation to attract the types of people who are more likely to buy from you.

You will also know, from experience, the length of time it takes for a prospect to enter this 'pipeline' and then pop out the other end as a customer. You'll know this because you've understood the sequence of decisions taken by your prospects and the time that it takes them to progress through those decisions. You'll know, for example, how long it takes your customers to use a pint of milk or update their car.

Let's say that for every 100 enquiries you receive, you win 10 orders, and that the average order value is £500. The total order value is £5,000, but to earn that £5,000, you have to deal with 90 enquiries which don't result in orders.

If the business requires an income of £3,000,000 per year, that means you have to bring in 6,000 orders per year, which is 500 orders per month, roughly 25 per working day. To win 25 orders a day, you have to deal with 250 enquiries. To do that, you need a big enough sales team, which increases your fixed and variable costs to the point where your profits decline.

Phew. It's not as easy as it looks. Certainly it's not as easy as just selling as much as you can.

Your turnover or sales target:	Your average order value:	How many orders you need, per:
		year
		month
		week
		day

Knowing your conversion ratios means that you know exactly what to focus on now to deliver the right income for the business tomorrow.

You'll know, for example, that if you don't have 100 people looking at your advert today, you won't be fitting carpets in 6 months time. Therefore, your focus should never be on chasing customers who might place an order, it should be on engaging with new prospects and then staying engaged with those prospects as they move along their decision process.

The time it takes a prospect to shuffle through your sales cycle is called the average sales cycle time, which is the time from the first point of contact with a prospect to the receipt of their order. In some businesses, this can be as long as 6 to 12 months, perhaps even longer, so if your income is falling, there's little that you can do that will impact it in the short term.

When income declines, every sales manager I've ever met wants the sales team to focus on the 'low hanging fruit', as in, the deals which are due to close shortly, or which can be closed shortly with a bit of pressure. You now know that the deals which are due to close shortly will close anyway, one way or the other, therefore the logical course of action is to sit tight and increase prospecting activities. No-one does that, though.

Knowing your conversion rates means that you can manage your activity now to deliver the right revenue in the future. It's the same in manufacturing; if something goes wrong at the start of the process, it's too late to do a quality check only at the end. You have to check quality at every stage of the production process, and in sales, we need to check quality, or conversions, at every stage too.

Clearly, the figures in the example above are unworkable with a team of 3 people, so let's work out what your actual ratios are.

7.1   Decision Points

List the decision points in your sales cycle, a point at which you have some form of contact with a prospect, at which that prospect makes a decision to move to the next stage or not.

enquiries   contacts   leads   orders

Sales Data   76

Just selling more is not a good way to increase profits. Because British Leyland miscalculated the production cost of the Mini in the 1970s, they made a small loss on each car sold. The Mini was very successful, so those small losses turned into big losses.

Once you know your decision points and conversion ratios, you know exactly what you need to do today to bring in orders tomorrow, next month and next year.

Good sales people spread the risk of the projects they are working on, so that they have a balance of short, medium and long sales cycles. Long sales cycles tend to mean that you're talking to the prospect before they are ready to buy, however that is useful because it 'locks out' your competitors and enables you to influence the buyer's decision. It's not going to pay the bills today, though, hence a balance is needed.

7.2   Conversion Ratios

Take the decision points from the previous exercise and put your own data into this table.

Decision Point	Qty per Day/ Week/ Month	Conversion Ratio

When you know your average order value, you can calculate how many prospects you need to be engaging with each day to generate the level of income that you need.

Target revenue:	Average order value:	Prospects per Day/Week/Month:

I was asked to deliver some sales coaching for a company that sold services to the health and fitness industry. They had one salesperson who only had to answer the phone because their events and online marketing generated incoming sales leads.

The owner of the business told me that they used to have a saleswoman who was fantastic, always on the phone, laughing and chatting with callers and, critically, winning lots of orders. She left, and the new guy just wasn't living up to their expectations. The owner's inclination was to fire him, but thought it only fair to give him some support first.

The salesman was making some obvious mistakes, but nothing really serious. For example, if a caller didn't decide to go ahead, he'd then ask for their contact details so that he could follow up. Of course, they made their excuses and said they'd call him, and he never heard from most of them again.

I got him to take their details as soon as they called on the pretence of being able to call them if they got cut off. At this point, the caller hasn't received the information they want, so they are more willing to trade their contact details in order to meet their particular needs.

This meant that he could then follow up, and of the people who he followed up with, some said no and some said, "I was just talking to my friend about you last night. You know, if I carry on procrastinating I'm never going to do this. Go on then, I'll go ahead." so his overall conversion rate improved.

This brings us to the fundamental problem in this story – the business owners only knew that they had a sales problem when they checked their bank balance. They had no idea how enquiries turned into money in the bank. By putting in place some very simple metrics and using those to tweak the salesman's behaviour, his performance steadily improved. After two weeks, we discovered something very interesting – he was outselling the 'fantastic' saleswoman by a considerable margin. He was by far a better salesperson than she had been. What this revealed was something the owners didn't know – the number if incoming leads had halved over the previous year. The new guy was getting close to her sales order value with half the number of leads. The owners realised they had to change their marketing in order to increase the number of leads. A specific issue that this highlighted was the activity of a new competitor who were taking market share from my client – again, something the owners hadn't noticed.

Their instinct, to look at the sales guy, wasn't necessarily misplaced, but their belief in his failure was. When I started working with him, his performance was just average. At the end of the four coaching sessions, his performance was outstanding. Yes, of course that was thanks to my brilliant coaching and considerable sales expertise. Alternatively, it was thanks to some simple metrics which showed us where the gaps were and what to do about them. The salesperson was just an average guy, which means that he was smart and efficient, a fast learner and able to focus on results.

Remember, you can't improve what you don't measure, simply because you won't know whether you've improved it or not.

8:   Prospecting

Prospecting is all of the activities you might undertake when finding potential customers.

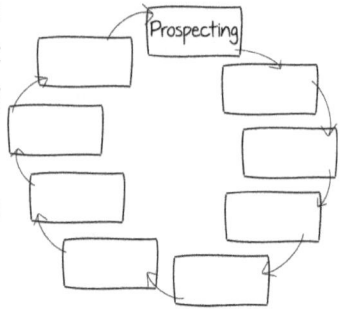

Prospecting activities can include:

- Cold calling

- Networking

- Social media

- Direct mail

- Advertising

- Joining trade networks

Each of these has a different cost, a different time requirement and a different rate of return. However, you can expect them all to have roughly the same cost of sale. If you find a prospecting method that gives you a significantly lower cost of sales then make the most of it while you can!

Targeted online advertising, for example, costs more on a pay-per-click basis than non-targeted advertising because you have to do less of it to reach the same number of qualified prospects.

Just because a prospecting method doesn't cost much doesn't make it cheap because the potentially lower conversion rate will make the cost of acquiring a new customer about the same.

What are the components of cost of sale?

When you add up these direct and indirect costs, you can see how much it costs you to earn every pound of income from sales.

A telemarketing agency that I knew ran a direct marketing campaign, making 2500 calls for a client with the objective of securing sales meetings.

2500
cold
calls ■

After making 2500 'cold calls', the agency secured 14 appointments. This is a conversion rate of 0.56% which is not bad for cold calling.

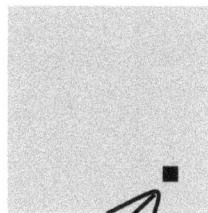

14 appointments

In 2010, it took 4 calls to reach a decision maker. In 2012, it took 41 calls. We are all increasingly exposed to sales messages, and we become naturally more resistant over time.

I'm not going to talk about specific cold calling techniques here, there are many books on that subject alone which you can read if that's a prospecting activity that you want to pursue. In this book, I want to convey an overall systematic approach to selling rather than focusing on techniques. What I will say is that cold calling doesn't work, or it does work, depending on whether it fits with your overall business model. What absolutely does not work is making ten cold calls, feeling disheartened and declaring cold calling to be a failure. With a 0.56% success rate, you can see that you need to make 179 calls to guarantee getting a meeting. That is a lot of calls. Let's say that the average call time is a minute, that's still three solid hours.

I would say that cold calling probably is more efficient for product sales than for service, because a product is easier for the prospect to understand and identify a need for. I know right away if I need new ink cartridges for my printer or new double glazing. However, if you're offering me car servicing or business consultancy then the chance of me needing that right now are slim. Actually, the chance of me needing double glazing right now is slim, which is why double glazing companies have such a bad reputation for their sales practices.

With a service, it's much harder for the prospect to get a good impression quickly through cold calling. Not impossible though, and because you'll be adopting a systematic approach to what you do, you'll try different angles and messages and measure what works best, rather than just using the trite and clichéd sales pitches out of a book. A different book, obviously.

8.1 Cold calling

Sooner or later, any salesperson has to pick up the telephone and call a potential customer. Many people call this 'cold calling' and this can make the process unnecessarily difficult for many sales people. It hardly sounds inviting, does it?

Whether you make sales calls from a list or to follow up on warm contacts from an introduction or networking event, at some point you do have to pick up the phone.

Some sales people excel at making sales calls, however many find it very hard. Whilst many sales people find it difficult to get into a routine with their sales calls, there is often a process that we can uncover using NLP modelling techniques.

For example, if you get variable results when making sales calls, you may have the right skills but an inconsistent process. If you get consistent but undesirable results, the process is working perfectly and it's the content you need to change.

Easily making sales calls is such an important aspect of the sales person's job that I'm going to share with you an article I wrote for a magazine on exactly this subject:

Making prospecting calls is one of the most important, and most feared parts of a sales person's job. The other day, I received this email from a sales person I worked with recently:

"I would just like to say a BIG, BIG thanks, I feel totally transformed, my 'phone fear' has disappeared. Its really quite weird, but I don't hesitate to pick the phone and ring people, in the past 10 days I've picked up 4-5 briefs. When I see an opportunity I just grab it.

I've noticed a big difference in my day too, I just don't know where the hours go, and I wish there were longer hours in the day to fit everything in. This will make you laugh, the last few days I've had lots of admin work, and haven't been able to get on the phone, I actually heard myself saying that 'I wish I was on the phone more' can you believe it?"

What would it be like if you felt the same way about your sales calls? Now, in order for you to be succeeding at your job, you must already be making sales calls, so I'm not talking about teaching you the basics here. I'm presuming you already do make calls, but maybe you tidy your desk, answer your emails and make a cup of coffee before you get yourself into the right mood. Maybe you stop after ten calls instead of stopping when the clients have all gone home. Maybe you make it harder for yourself than it needs to be.

Maybe you already love sales calls and you're already getting great results, in which case – why are you reading this? Get on the phone!

A change like this can happen very quickly. The longest this has ever taken was about an hour, the shortest about one minute.

But how? Well, the exact process varies from one person to the next because every person I've ever worked with creates this situation in a slightly different, unique way – and so will you. Having said that, there are some general principles and patterns that I can tell you about that you can use right away to improve your approach and therefore your results.

Firstly, stop cold calling. It's difficult, time consuming and produces poor results. Instead, spend some time each day calling people you haven't spoken to before and finding out how you can help them.

Secondly, At the moment you pick up the phone to dial, what picture pops into your head? What does the voice in your head say? Do you begin your call by apologising, or does your voice tone demonstrate the pride you take in your job? Just work through these simple steps, giving yourself time to think this through very carefully:

Imagine yourself sitting at your desk at the time you would begin making sales calls. As you imagine starting to dial, what picture pops into your head. Specifically, whose picture? If you find sales calls consistently difficult, I'm guessing the picture is of someone you don't have much in common with who doesn't look pleased to hear from you. If you find calls randomly difficult, I'm guessing there's no coherent picture. In either case, that's good news.

Next, imagine you're about to call your best friend or someone you like very, very much. You know exactly what I mean. As you dial, what picture pops into your mind? Now, stop and think about yourself – are you smiling? Are you sitting upright? Are you dialling eagerly? When you speak, does your tone of voice reflect this?

So, if you imagine someone who doesn't want to talk to you, simply imagine reaching out and grabbing the picture, screwing it into a ball and throwing it over your shoulder. Then simply draw a new picture of someone who looks like you, who you have something in common with and who looks pleased to hear from you, or at least open minded. Imagine calling that person and notice how your voice tone is different.

Practice this a few times, repeating the process over and over. Imagine starting to dial, see the face of someone you want to talk to, hear your positive voice tone, notice how that feels nice to talk to someone who enjoys talking to you.

Thirdly, what do you say to yourself before, during and after the call? If it's in any way critical that's not helping. Often, the voice in your head has really valuable feedback but you don't hear it because it just sounds like nagging or criticism. Think again about sitting down to make your calls and this time pay attention to what you are saying to yourself. Change the voice tone to something more neutral, like a news reader, or to a voice that you like – even something sexy! Now, listen to what the voice tells you – is the information more useful? You can also ask questions back. If the voice is critical, say, "Thank you! Now, how does that information help me?" or, "Thank you! Now, what do you suggest I do differently?" Oddly enough, you'll find the same approach works very well with that person in the office who always offers you helpful criticism.

Last of all, you can't really control what happens during each call as you are not in control of the person at the other end. They might be busy or tired and you know the importance of respecting their state. So, no matter how each call goes, it's important to treat each call as if it's your first. There are many ways that you can quickly control your state, and the simplest for our purposes here is through your focus of attention. Think of a time in the past when you felt really confident and in control of yourself. Remember that time in all the detail you can, recalling what you saw, heard and felt. Maybe you even remember some smells and tastes. When you have all that, think of a word, colour or piece of music that seems to represent it. Repeat this a few times so that the trigger becomes associated with the feeling. Now, in between calls simply replay the trigger and your state will switch to the confident, in control state.

After you have practised all this for a day and then slept on it, your brain will build it into an unconscious calling routine for you so you won't even have to think in order to get good results. What's this based on? The principle that you are already following an unconscious process which is working perfectly for you. The process is fine but the results need a little tweak. By taking conscious control over the process and making some slight adjustments, you'll find that you can get surprising results, very quickly. How quickly? You'll only find out by finding out!

8.2   Social Media

Social media websites are valuable prospecting tools. LinkedIn is currently the best tool to use, but you should also make the most of the social features of sites more relevant to your customers.

When you make contact with a new customer, you can invite them to LinkedIn or to like your Facebook page. Use it to keep track of what they're doing, who they're talking to and to send them regular updates about developments or events that might interest them.

You can also use LinkedIn to find new prospects by searching within companies or industries, or looking through the connections of your colleagues and even your competitors.

8.3   Networking Events

Local networking events are as popular as ever, with everyone from professional bodies and universities to local law firms and business clubs getting together on a regular basis. I've found that many of these events are attended by small business owners, hoping to find customers, which is absolutely not the right approach to take.

For a start, you need to only attend events which are very relevant to you and your business. That's obvious, but it reveals an interesting point about these events – that many people who attend them do so, not to extend their networks, but because they're lonely. And when you're lonely, any event will do, and if you can find like minded people there, to gripe about how bad things are, you'll find the experience reassuring, if not productive.

Your purpose for attending such an event is not to complain, and it's certainly not to sell because the chances of finding your ideal customer at the moment they're ready to buy is highly unlikely. Not impossible, just highly unlikely. Some events are free to attend, some charge. The ones where you're most likely to find a potential customer charge the most, of course!

9:   Qualifying

Good sales people value
their time, so they
qualify every sales lead
to make sure it's worth
investing in.

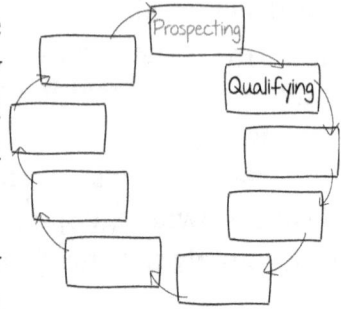

Even if you have plenty
of time to deal with
every lead, you still need to qualify them because
otherwise you are wasting time that you could be
spending doing something more valuable.

In order to be able to qualify each lead or
prospect, you have to know what you want out of
a customer. Just because they have a requirement
for an engineering service doesn't mean that they
will definitely buy *your* service.

9.1   Ideal Customer

Define your ideal customer.

When you know your ideal customer, you can qualify every lead with a set of questions and make an informed decision about how to deal with that lead.

9.2   Qualification Criteria

In sales, these questions are called qualification criteria. They don't automatically rule a lead in or out, they just give you information on which to make a decision that is right for the business at that time. If enquiries are slow, you might apply the criteria less ruthlessly than when you're overloaded and you need to prioritise. Without qualification criteria, you can't ever prioritise based on what's good for the business, so you'll tend to prioritise based on what you like doing most, or on who is shouting the loudest.

One thing that I can tell you about qualification is that any sale that you will ever lose, any sale that any salesperson has ever lost, can be identified at the qualification stage. You'll spend months working on a deal, only to find that the prospect has no budget set aside, or not enough budget, or they have an interest but not a specific need, or there's no compelling event and so they end up waiting... and waiting... and waiting.

There will only ever be one reason for you to lose a deal, and that's because someone else had more information than you did, someone else asked the tough qualification questions that you were afraid to ask.

If the prospect doesn't have a compelling event, or budget, do you ignore them? Not necessarily, but you do prioritise accordingly and, most importantly, you focus only on the next decision point and not on the getting the final order.

We're going to define a custom set of qualification criteria just for you, and they might include:

- Decision Maker - Is the person you're talking to able to make a buying decision?

- Time - How much of your time is it going to take to win the order?

- Budget - Can the customer realistically afford your service?

- Ability to Pay - Is the customer's business financially stable?

- Need - Does the customer have a clear need for your service?

- Solution - Are you able to solve the customer's problem?

- Cost of Sale / Margin - Is there enough profit to make it worthwhile?

- Effort – Will you need to invest so much time and resource that you're better off doing something else?

- Competition - Do you know who else the customer is talking to?

- Compelling event – Why now?

9.3   Define Your Qualification Criteria

Criteria	Definition

You could even make your criteria into an acronym or mnemonic if you like. The first one I learned, back in 1992, was NETWORKS:

- Need
- Effort
- Timescale
- Who
- Original
- Reason
- Kompetition (sic)
- Solution

For the consultants who had trouble with cold calling, I came up with TEAMWIN, which was a play on their company name:

- Timescale
- Effort
- Authority
- Money
- Who else?
- Interest
- Need

10: Opening

Many sales people struggle to close a sale. They might get into a comfortable, technical conversation with the customer, or they might be enjoying talking about golf so much that it feels uncomfortable to change the direction of the conversation and ask for the order.

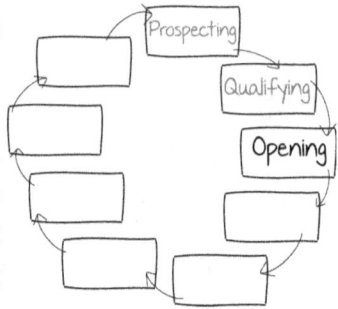

The solution to this is very simple; if you want to close a sales process, you first have to open it.

As a salesperson, you need to drive the conversation from the very beginning.

Opening the sales process means that you are setting the goals and the boundaries for the conversation. You're essentially saying, "I'm talking to you because I can provide a solution to your problem, and at the end of our conversation I expect you to make a decision to buy my solution or not."

10.1   This Isn't a Sales Call...

Some sales people think that customers don't like being sold to, so they respond by pretending that they're not sales people. They're consultants, or advisers, or they're just checking they have the right details for you.

The problem is that when you start a call by disguising the reason for the call, all you end up doing is confusing and aggravating the customer. By being clear and honest, you encourage the customer to make an instant decision about whether they're interested in talking to you or not, and either is good.

One of the most effective ways to learn the difference between good and bad sales calls is to actually receive incoming sales calls. If someone makes a bad impression on you, take a moment to think about why. Similarly, if someone does something good, make a note of it.

The problem with sales calls that don't go well is that you have created a poor first impression that is almost impossible to undo. The biggest obstacle to sales calls is that customers don't have a lot of time, so if they don't have time for the first call you make, they're certainly not going to have time for you to explain why you didn't make a good impression the first time.

The earlier you give the customer a decision to make, the more you can influence their decisions. Many sales people are afraid of giving the customer a decision, because they're afraid that the customer will say no. However, the best sales people know that the earlier the customer says no the better, because that frees up their time to find a customer who will say yes. If your service isn't relevant to the customer, there's absolutely nothing to be gained from manipulating them into letting you send them a brochure.

Surprisingly, the most effective opening for an outgoing call is often:

"This is a sales call, do you have two minutes?"

Since time is the single most precious asset of any customer or salesperson, the best sales call is one where you get to the point, quickly, and help the prospect to make an instant decision. Acting decisively actually makes it easier for the prospect to say 'yes', because you shorten the time within which the prospect feels uncomfortable because they don't know what you want. By getting the prospect's attention right at the start with clarity and honesty, you gain their 'buy in' to the conversation, which means that they are more likely to want to hear you out. Remember that the prospect is making a series of decisions which began even before you spoke to them – they decided to answer the phone. They listened to your opening, and then they decided to keep on listening. The decided to either engage with you or put the phone down. They decided that they wanted to hear more. Each decision builds on the previous one, and the more decisions that the prospect makes, the more committed they become to a course of action. Therefore, the best opening is one that gets the prospect to make a decision, such as, "(opening pitch) do you have two minutes to discuss that now and decide if you want to then hear more?"

I'm not saying that this is the perfect opening for you to use, what I'm saying is that you must concentrate on the process of sales, not the magic words. The process will give you the right words.

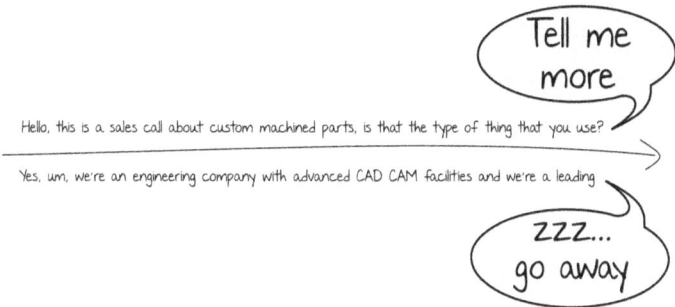

Exactly the same applies to an incoming enquiry call. While the customer instigates the call, you must take control of the call right away by asking questions.

Whatever the customer's enquiry, there are certain things that you need to know; what they are interested in, delivery requirements, the problem that the customer is trying to solve, the impact of that problem and so on.

As soon as you have control of the conversation, you can ask questions which move back through the customer's decision process, so even if they start by giving you a technical requirement, you can very quickly move the conversation to a higher level, which increases the perceived value of your solution.

However, the starting point of any incoming conversation is to find out why the prospect is calling.

When the prospect launches into their questions, it can seem difficult, even rude, to say, "Whoa! Hold on there, let me ask the questions first!", so we really need to find a more subtle way to take control of the conversation.

As you'll see shortly, when the phone rings, that might be your first interaction with that prospect but it is not their first interaction with you. Something made them pick up the phone, therefore they have a clear outcome for the conversation – or at least they think they do. They think that they want to either ask some questions or place an order. The problem is that the answers you give them might not be what they were expecting, and they won't be able to move closer to a decision.

Remember that when you answer the phone, the prospect is at a decision point, and they are calling you because they cannot make that decision by themselves. They either need information for their decision, or they need you to act on their decision. Either way, they are calling you because they cannot move forwards to resolve their situation without speaking to you, or someone who they think is like you such as your competitors.

If I call 3 different carpet shops to get a price, I expect to have 3 identical conversations. If you are the only person to ask me a particular question, or offer a suggestion, then you have shifted the balance of the conversation and you will therefore be more valuable to me than someone who just gives me what I ask for.

10.2　What Do You Want?

"Why are you calling?" might sound a little abrupt, and the customer probably thinks that the reason they're calling is obvious. However, their reason, as in their expected outcome, is not obvious. They might be calling because:

- They want to get a price

- They want some free advice

- They want to fish for competitive information

- They want to place an order

- They're bored

Once you know why the customer is calling, you can find out what it is they need.

However, before we get into gathering needs, we should find out more about the buying decision itself, because we want to make sure that we keep control of this as a sales conversation before it becomes a technical conversation, which is easy, but doesn't lead to an order.

Remember that the reason for every call that you make or receive, and for every meeting that you attend, is to move the prospect one step closer to a decision.

- What do you want to get out of this conversation?

- Are you aiming to place an order today?

- What information do you need to make a decision?

- Have you spoken to anyone else?

- Have you had any other prices?

- Have you bought something like this before?

- Are you likely to need more of these in the future?

- Do you need to open a credit account?

- Can you tell me a little about your business?

- Do you have a website?

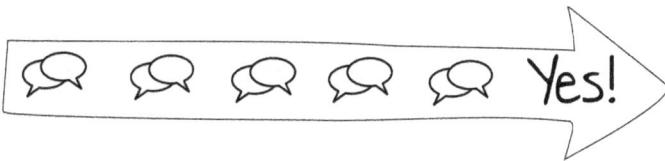

The technical discussion then becomes one part of the overall process, one step on the journey.

10.3 Taking Control

Take control of the conversation as early as you can by asking questions. Based on your experience of the enquiries you receive, write down some opening questions that you can use.

Even with a set of wonderful questions to hand, you still might find it difficult to get a word in sideways and get control. The more work the prospect has done before calling you, the more specific they will be in what they ask you for.

If I've measured my living room, chosen the colour, make and product name of a carpet, I'll ring a shop, give them the specification and ask for a price including fitting. Where can they go from there? How can they add value? I've left them no room to negotiate, so they have to try and open up the process again. This seems difficult, countless sales trainers and books make it sound very complicated, and in practice it is so easy that you will fall off your chair when I tell you. Therefore, please sit on the floor now, surrounded by cushions or soft colleagues, to prevent injury and damage to property. Most importantly, put the book on a flat, stable surface so that you don't drop it.

Here's a clue for you. When you answered the phone, you had control of the conversation, and you immediately gave that control to the prospect.

How did you do that?

You invited them to speak.

"Hello, ABC Engineering, how can I help?"

How can I help. How, indeed. Where shall I begin?

The caller will tell you exactly how you can help, because you just asked them to. You gave them control.

Here's a very slightly different alternative greeting, I suggest you try them both and see what happens for yourself.

"Hello, ABC Engineering, my name is Pat, can I take your name please? Thank you Joe, and can I take your phone number in case we get cut off? Great. How can I help you, Joe?"

The pattern of the first example is:

You've dialled the right number, you can have whatever you want.

The pattern of the second example is:

You've dialled the right number, I'll give you some information, then you give me some information, and you get what you want when I invite you to.

The first example is an invitation for the prospect to get what they want – a one way transaction.

The second example is an invitation to trade – a two way transaction.

You take control of the conversation by not giving it away in the first place!

When the prospect calls you, they are not calling you out of the blue because they have nothing better to do. They are calling you in response to something you have done. You put your phone number in a directory, or on your business card, or on your website, asking people to call you.

They are not calling you, they are replying to you. They are accepting your invitation.

I urge you to try out both greetings, and experiment with others too. Based on my own research, the pattern I've noticed is this:

Salesperson:	Good morning, ABC, how can I help?
Customer:	I want to order ... Can you tell me how much ...

Salesperson:	Good morning, ABC, my name is ... can I take your name? ... and your number ... and how can I help you, Sam?
Customer:	I'm looking for ... I need some help with ...

Can you see the pattern? Simply by making the conversation a two-way trade rather than a one-way reaction, the prospect changes from saying what they *want* to saying what they are *doing*.

This might seem like such an insignificant change, so let me spell it out for you a bit more.

When you open with, "How can I help?" the prospect will take your invitation literally. When the prospect tells you what they want you to do to help them, they expect you to give them only what they ask for.

Since you are then reacting to the prospect, you'll tend to ask for their contact details to "follow up" at the end of the call, if at all.

At the end of the call, the prospect has what they wanted, so why should they give you anything in return? You were happy to give them the information they needed for free, so they want the call to be over as quickly as possible.

When you go shopping, after you pay for your purchases, do you hang around in the shop afterwards? What happens if the retailer puts their 'bargain shelf' after the checkouts, as some DIY chains do?

How is IKEA the exception to this? What do IKEA place after their checkouts?

Ice creams, soft drinks and hot dogs. Why are these treats *after* the checkouts? Why even have them at all when you've already passed the café upstairs. Because as I said, they are treats, a reward for shopping. You have been a good little girl or buy, here is an ice cream.

When you slow the conversation down and open by trading information, you will hear the prospect respond differently. When the prospect tells you what they are doing, they are telling you about their current situation, opening up space for you to ask questions and make suggestions.

Try it both ways and see what happens.

I'll close this section with one of the easiest and most ridiculously obvious ways to gain control of the conversation. Firstly, remember that you already have control, because you chose to answer the phone, so don't give it away by asking "How can I help?" before you've captured their contact details. So this leads to the obvious question, how do you capture their contact details? You need to record them in some way, yes? Let's assume you're not using a fancy bit of software to do that, and instead you're resorting to a legacy CRM system – the notepad and pen.

"Let me just grab a notepad... OK, thank you, my name is Sam, can I take your name? ..."

The obvious part? You already had your pen and notepad in front of you.

10.4   Email Enquiries

When you receive an email enquiry, the first thing you have to do is call the customer. Assume that they have emailed all of your competitors, and that they can all provide the same service at the same price. The most important factor in winning the business therefore isn't the quality of your response but the **speed**.

Speed is important because the first supplier to respond to the customer sets the benchmark by which all other suppliers will be measured.

If you don't already have them, put together some proposal templates for common services so that you can respond with a high quality proposal, quickly.

As a rough guide, you should aim to call a customer within **10** minutes of them making an enquiry, and have some information to them within **30** minutes. If you can't send a proposal because you're waiting for information, at least send what you can; a description of your services, case studies etc.

Whatever you do, remember that the supplier who responds first sets the bar.

10.5   The Most Important Question

For an inbound enquiry, there is one question which is even more important than, "Why?", and that question is:

"Why now?"

Consider the chain of events:

Customer makes enquiry	Customer receives information	Customer makes decision to buy	Customer receives product or service

Is that what really happens? From your point of view, it might, because that is the window through which you see the customer interaction.

Here's the same chain of events from the customer's point of view:

Something happens
Customer has a need
Customer looks for information to fulfil their need
Customer makes enquiry
Customer receives information
Customer makes decision to buy
Customer receives product or service
Customer uses product or service

If we are to generate maximum sales from inbound enquiries, we **must** find out what has made the customer call now, rather than yesterday or tomorrow. The customer has taken action because **something has changed**. In sales, we call that the 'compelling event', and we have to find out what that is.

The customer is not calling to buy your product or service, they are calling to solve their problem, and they are calling **now** because they have the problem **now**.

If you aren't relating your product or service to the customer's problem, you have no way of making yourself stand out from all of your competitors.

11:   Needs

Establishing the customer's needs is much more than getting a list of requirements from them. That tells you what the customer is asking for, and I can say that in nearly 30 years, the only times that I've seen customers with purple faces, threatening legal action, is when the salesperson sold them what they asked for instead of what they needed.

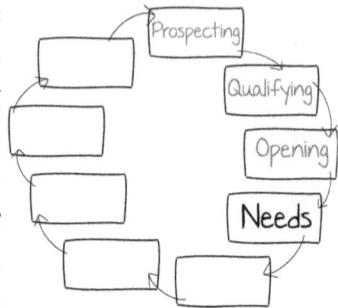

Working to understand the customer's needs doesn't just tell you what they want you to supply to them; it also helps you to understand what they're going to do with it, so that you can:

- Suggest alternatives

- Offer advice

- Warn the customer of any potential problems

- Identify new sales opportunities

- Build perceived value in your solution

To discover a customer's needs, you have to ask questions. A stereotypical view of sales people is that they are talkative, good at telling people how wonderful their products are. In fact, the best sales people talk much less than you might think; instead, they are good at getting the customer talking. And of course, the way that they do that is by asking questions.

An old saying is...

Telling is not Selling

By far the most effective way to sell to a customer is to ask questions.

Questions are very important because they enable you to:

- Gather vital information

- Check understanding

- Take control of the conversation

If you don't take control of the conversation then the caller will be in control, they will only ask for the information that they think they need and they will be unlikely to give you anything in return.

As you now know, the sales process is a series of trades. If the caller wants information from you, they have to give you information in return.

11.1 Gathering Needs

As soon as you have control of the conversation, you can ask questions which move back through the customer's decision process, so even if they start by giving you a detailed requirement, you can very quickly move the conversation to a 'higher level', which increases the perceived value of your solution.

- What do you need?

- What are you hoping that will do for you?

- Have you looked at other suppliers?

What exactly do we mean by conversing at a 'higher level'? Quite simply, all you're really doing is moving the conversation back to the previous decision point in order to broaden it out and prevent yourself from being rail-roaded into the customer's idea of what will solve their problem.

There are many different methodologies for gathering needs, but all you really have to bear in mind is the question, "So what?"

I want a new carpet. So what?

What a prospect wants is not necessarily what they need. As a child you probably wanted ice cream for breakfast, but it's not what you needed. I want a new carpet, but I don't need one. Whatever people say they want is often very different to what they need, and what they go on to buy.

If you ask your prospects to tell you what they want, they will tend to give you a shopping list of the features they'd like, and when you tell them the price they fall off their chairs.

If you ask what they need, you may get a different answer, but it might not be very different.

If we move back to the previous decision point then we're talking about the problem that created the need.

If we move to the decision point before that, we're talking about the compelling event that created the problem which created the need which resulted in the conversation.

List some useful questions for gathering needs.

11.2   Recording Information

It's important to have a consistent way of recording the information that you gather, for at least two reasons:

- It makes you ask the questions that you might otherwise miss

- Everyone knows where to find information about a customer's enquiry

Let's design an enquiry form to use with every customer. If an enquiry comes in by email, the first thing to do is call the customer to "confirm a few more details" so you can use this form for either inbound calls or email follow-ups.

11.3   Checking you Understand

Once you've gathered the customer's needs, you need to check that you understand them.

When the customer is talking through their ideas and requirements, they're rarely doing so in a structured way. When you take control of the conversation, you create that structure.

The simplest way to check understanding is to read back what you've heard to the customer.

Let me check that I understand you correctly...

When you check your understanding in this way, the customer can say one of two things:

- Yes

- No

If they say yes, you've understood them. If they say no, you can explore what you didn't understand. Not rocket science.

In the old days, communication skills training courses used to advocate showing understanding by paraphrasing. This is probably still being taught today, and it's generally a bad idea, because when you change someone's words you're changing the meaning. Your objective is to demonstrate that you understand them, not to get them to understand you. Paraphrasing changes the customer's meaning and breaks the rapport that you have developed with them.

"I want a new mobile phone with a big screen and good speakers and a long battery life."

"So you're saying that you would like to upgrade your phone to something with a much better specification?"

"Erm, no, what I said is..."

Some people say that if you only repeat back the customer's words, you are only showing that you listened, not that you understood. I say that if you paraphrase, you are describing what you think their words meant to you, which probably isn't what their words meant to them.

You won't believe me until you've tried it for yourself, so I have devised an exercise which I use during training courses. Here's a transcript of the exercise from a series of training courses for 250 sales people who wanted to be better at getting access to high level decision makers.

Years ago, sales people used to be trained to make small talk with customers. There were sales people who had intimate knowledge of their customers' families, hobbies and golf handicaps, yet they didn't sell anything. We learn by making connections, and those connections often take the form of a purpose. For example, you know what a sandwich is for, so you know how to know when you need one. We do this with relationships, too especially those brief, fleeting relationships that we experience in business. We remember people by what the relationship is for. Guess what? If the customer remembers you as that nice person he talks to about golf, he will come to you for exactly that. If he thinks about your relationship in the context of buying your products and services, that's what track his mind will switch onto when you meet or talk. And if he thinks of you as someone who helps him to solve real business problems... well you can guess the rest. The important thing here is context, so right from the very first meeting, you need to keep your conversation within the context of his business and his business problems – problems that you are going to help him solve.

When people make decisions, their words only rationalise a decision that has already been made, emotionally. By tuning into those emotional signals, you'll know what the customer wants before he does. If the customer has an emotional response to something, that's a good sign that it is important! If you challenge that decision or opinion head on with facts and figures, all you're doing is embedding the customer deeper into that emotional response. In short, your efforts to change their mind actually convince them more.

I know what you're thinking – "show me how!" By the way, as well as being able to read minds, you can also use these ideas to improve the quality of your personal relationships too!

OK, let's practice something really simple first. In a moment I'm going to ask you to pair up and do a really quick exercise – 5 minutes each is plenty of time for this.

What I want you to do is have your partner tell you about a current, real problem they have that they feel some emotional connection to – maybe frustration, disappointment, confusion, whatever.

You may want to get your notepad and right now, think of a problem you currently have and make a note of it. It can be anything at all – whatever you have in mind write now.

As they tell you about it I want you to ignore their words completely. I know that, as nosey human beings, we like to get tied up in the content, offer suggestions, fix people's problems and so on. Irritating, when people do that to you instead of listening, isn't it! I want you to completely ignore their words and instead focus on only three things, and I want you to notice what they do when they talk about a particular aspect of the problem, or experience a particular emotional state. What I want you to pay attention to is:

- Their voice tone
- Where they look
- What they do with their hands

That's all there is to it! So, really quickly pair up and I'll call you back in just over 10 minutes. When you're done, stay with your partner for the second part of the exercise.

Feedback from the audience included points such as:

I couldn't pay attention to all 3 aspects, only 1 or 2

Every time my partner said x he did y

I found it hard to not listen to content

He looked around a lot

She moved her hands a lot

His voice tone changed when he talked about his feelings

Excellent. You've noticed some really good things there, the kind of things that really excellent communicators notice intuitively. Now we'll do part two of that exercise.

Go back to the person you worked with last time and summarise their problem back to them to check your understanding.

I want you to each play back your partner's problem, concentrating on using the exact voice tone they used, looking where they looked (as if they were looking at something real) and moving your hands in the same way. If they showed you a direction, or an obstacle, or a picture, just reflect that back. You don't have to understand what it means, you're just respecting the fact that it means something to them. Don't try to understand or summarise the problem at this point. So play back your partner's problem concentrating on their voice tone, eye movement and gestures.

Each take a turn to do that, and again you only need a couple of minutes each.

Feedback from the audience included:

I felt like my partner was really listening

I felt comfortable with my partner

I felt that my partner really understood me

I was surprised that I do all of that when I talk

My partner was very perceptive

What you have done by noticing your partner's voice tone, eye movements and gestures is pick up on the key non verbal communication channels. You have started to focus on the 93% of communication where someone's true beliefs, reactions and intentions are communicated. By focusing on those three things, you will pick up far more valuable information than all of the business plans and organisation charts in the world will tell you.

I think it's a bit unfair that we should spend time exploring your problems and not let you solve them, so the final thing we're going to do is solve a problem only by asking questions about it. Remember, it's not your problem so it's not your responsibility to solve it. All you need to do is change your partner's perspective of the problem.

Think about this in a customer scenario. When you are talking to a customer who is telling you about a business problem, it matters. It means something to him because he has an emotional response to it. As you're learning during this workshop, the problem isn't really about software compatibility, user capacity or even customer satisfaction. The problem is about emotions – triggered by politics, power, threats, perceptions, promotions and so on. If you sit in front of your customer and really listen in the way you have practised here today, you will create a greater depth of rapport and empathy than you can imagine. The problem with this is that the customer will automatically associate you with the problem – specifically, just because he has told you about it and you have listened, he will think you can solve it.

So let's try out a few questions that we can use to clarify the problem. These questions work in a particular way, changing your partner's perception of the problem. When their perception changes, they will see solutions that had previously been hidden from them. I want you to question the problem using only the questions on the slide. It doesn't matter if you ask the same question more than once, you will get a different answer each time as the problem changes.

If your partner says something that has "I can't" in it, reply with "What would happen if you did?"

You have 5 minutes each for this – and if you solve the problem with the first question, just talk about whatever you like! Remember to ask these questions gently, as if you really care about the person's problem, and as if you know that they already know how to solve it, they just haven't realised it yet.

- What is important to you about solving this?

- Imagine it's a year from now, what has changed?

- Imagine it's a month from now, how does it feel different?

- What stops you from solving this now?

- What would happen if you did?

- What does a good solution look, sound and feel like?

- What do you really want to do about this?

- Think of someone who would handle this really well. What would they do?

Feedback from the audience included:

It really helped me to think through the problem

It helped me to find my own solution

It changed my perspective of the problem

I feel differently about the problem

Now, you might be thinking that this is all very well for face to face meetings, what about the times when you call someone over the phone? Well, it's exactly the same with just a small difference. This 93% of communication that is unconscious is made up of two components – visual and auditory – which need to reinforce each other for communication to be 'congruent'. We normally perceive congruence as confidence, certainty or honesty. When we speak to someone over the telephone, we only have the auditory component, so where does the visual component come from? We make it up! We make it up based on our own expectations, and on the auditory component.

When you're making sales calls, you unconsciously visualise the person you are calling. If you have never met them, you visualise something based on your prior experience. This is why calls often go exactly the way you intend them to – when you're feeling confident the call goes well, when you are nervous and doubting yourself, the call goes badly.

You've all done so well that I think we should wrap up this part of the workshop with one final exercise, that will take you only a couple of minutes each. I want you to use only your intuition for this. I know you all have a strong intuition, and I know how aware you are of what happens when you trust it, and what happens when you don't. With your partner, I want you to simply trust your intuition. Don't rationalise it, don't explain it, don't find reasons for it. Just tell your partner what you feel their problem is really all about, and give them one single piece of advice. Don't sit there and analyse it. Don't worry about whether it is right or wrong. It doesn't have to make any sense. Just say what you feel is right.

Feedback from the audience included:

The summary was absolutely spot on

My partner discovered something really important that I hadn't even mentioned

The suggestion was really accurate

My partner told me what I already knew I had to do

You see, the 93% and 7% don't just work in the way we communicate outwards – they also apply to the way we take information in. What you have just done, by trusting your intuition, is allowed yourself access to more of your brain than just by focusing analytically. So if you really want to pay attention to someone, stop listening and allow yourself to really hear.

We've got time for one last exercise, so let's put together everything you have learned so far. I want you to pair up again and imagine that you're making a telephone call to someone who you want to arrange a meeting with. You can do this exercise with your eyes closed if you really want to simulate being on the telephone – that's up to you.

What I want you to do is think of two people now. The first is someone who you find difficult or obstructive, who you struggle to communicate with and who never gives you what you ask for. The second is someone who you get on well with, someone who you feel is always helpful and always sounds pleased to hear from you.

What you're going to do is randomly pick one of those two people and really imagine that you are about to call them to arrange a meeting. Imagine what they look like, imagine their voice and imagine how you feel when you are preparing to talk to them.

As you imagine that person, imagine you are calling them and when they answer, tell your partner whatever you normally say when you make a call. It's not a role play, so your partner does not have to pretend to be that person – you just say whatever you normally say as you imagine talking to the person you have chosen.

Do this a few times, each time selecting one of your two people at random and taking a moment to really imagine talking to them.

Your partner's role is very simple – just listen carefully and guess which person your partner is thinking of. After they have made a few 'calls' tell them what differences you noticed.

Feedback from the audience included:

It was really obvious!

My partner was convinced there was no difference, but I heard it right away

My partner's nervous voice tone made me feel nervous

My partner's confidence made me feel really receptive

My partner's aggression made me feel intimidated

We've worked with lots of sales people, helping them to really enjoy making sales calls. One common thing that sales people do is to imagine the person they're calling being impatient or even rude, so they're apologising even before the other person picks up the phone. The solution is to simply imagine you're calling someone you look forward to talking to! The difference in your voice tone will make a huge difference to the state and response of the person you're calling.

So, during this part of the workshop, what have we achieved? Well, instead of hearing just 7% of the customer's communication, through their words, we have started to focus on 100% of their communication. It's in that hidden 93% that what they are really trying to tell you is conveyed. By paying attention to that, you will learn more about what is really important to them, and that creates greater empathy and strengthens the connection between you. That strong connection allows you to ask questions that normally you wouldn't get away with, and those questions help you to change the person's perception. Changing the other person's perceptions is the basis for changing their opinions, needs and beliefs, and that is the basis for creating a powerful business relationship.

Through these simple ideas, you can build stronger relationships, influence state and you can change people's minds. You can understand people like never before, and they will want to tell you about what is important to them, because they feel good about telling you. What more could you want!

11.4 What's it worth?

You've listened to your customer with baited breath and now you understand their needs intimately. So what? You know what they need. Big deal. So just sell them that then.

The risk you now face is that it's too easy just to give your customer what they're asking for.

A popular sales training model developed by Neil Rackham is SPIN. While observing sales people, he noticed that the best ones asked a lot of questions to help them develop a picture of the customers background situation, their problems and what those problems meant in terms of impact to the business. The final question was to understand what those problems were costing the customer's business, so that a 'value proposition' could be made, a proposal with a direct connection between the cost impact of the problem and the cost benefit of the solution.

"So if I could solve the problem of your unreliable photocopier which costs you £100 a year with a brand new photocopier that costs only £100 then after a year you will be saving yourself £100 a year, is that something you would be interested in?"

Obviously, this idea was introduced when £100 was a lot of money. And when there were such things as photocopiers.

The point is that if you don't know what your customers needs mean to them in financial terms, you have no foundation on which to build value. Your carefully extracted needs will just be a shopping list for the customer to use to compare you to your competitors.

When you uncover your customers' needs using the method I described above, not only will you understand your customer, you will have developed a far deeper connection with them which cannot easily be replicated by your competitors. And if your customer is spending time with you, they will be less likely to want to repeat themselves to other suppliers, which gives you a competitive advantage.

12: Building Value

When you decide to buy
something, you compare
what the item **costs** and
what you feel it is **worth**.

Retailers manipulate this
process with discounts
and special offers, and
'daily deals' websites manipulate this still further
with daily offers of perhaps 70% off the price of
something. Unfortunately, they are also playing
on your tendency to over-value things that are in
limited supply. If you took a few minutes to
check other sites, you'd find that you can buy the
same thing elsewhere for less than the
discounted price.

Customers raise price objections because your
price is higher than their expectations, and their
expectations are in turn based on their decision
process. If you don't influence that process, you
have no choice but to negotiate on price.

What are the features of your service that
warrant a higher than market price?

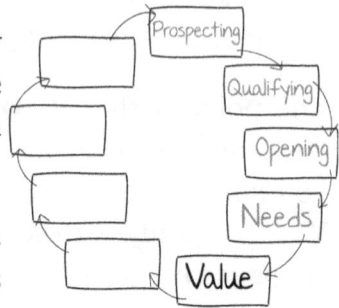

- Time

- Relationship

- Quality

- Service

- Availability

- Expertise

- Uniqueness

- Anything else?

Building value in your solution means putting a price on what it's worth to the customer to have their problem solved.

This will change the customer's response from, "£100?? You must be joking!" to "£100 to solve my problem, that's good value!"

As I mentioned previously, first you have to figure out what the customer's unfulfilled needs are currently costing them.

We know that value is subjective, so it will change in comparison to other factors. Fuel is more expensive on the motorway or at the last service station before the middle of nowhere, and water is more expensive in the desert.

A customer will make a decision that they feel most comfortable with when the price that they have to pay becomes equivalent to the value that they will get from the product or service.

When we feel coerced into paying too high a price, perhaps for a house where we thought there was a lot of competition from other buyers, we don't feel good about the decision, and we are unlikely to recommend the supplier to our friends. Similarly, when we feel we've paid too low a price, perhaps for a house where our first offer was readily accepted, we also don't feel good about the decision. We are happiest when we feel fairly treated.

13: Solution

We've now reached the stage in the sales cycle where you tell the customer what you propose to sell them. You might do this verbally, or you might send a written proposal.

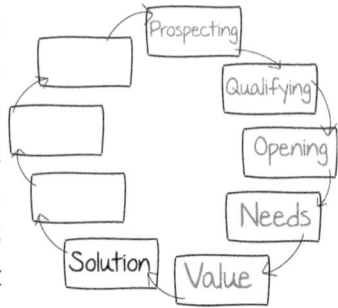

We'll come on to the proposal format shortly, but first let's look at one of the most typical things you'll hear sales people talk about; Features and Benefits.

A **feature** is an aspect, quality or characteristic of a product or service.

A **benefit** is a reason why that feature would be useful for a customer.

A feature of this handbook is that it is *white*. The benefit to you is that it's *easy to read*.

Almost all sales people are trained to described features and benefits using the phrase "which means that..."

"This book is white which means that it's easy to read"

This is the wrong way round, as it creates a break in 'rapport', the sense of harmony and common ground that you have created with your customer.

A better way is to use the word "because..."

"This book is easy to read because it's printed on white paper"

Perhaps you're already aware of how your mind runs ahead of what other people are saying to you, filling in the blanks ahead of them. If they are talking slowly, it's easy to get frustrated because you want them to get to the point. This happens because we comprehend language at a number of levels, and each level has a number of possibilities. Your brain is able to make sense of language by trying to predict these possibilities. At the most basic level, the sound of a word might be ambiguous, and until you hear more context, it's difficult to work out the correct meaning.

The words right, write and rite all sound the same but have very different meanings. Even 'right' is ambiguous.

Saying "Feature which means that benefit" makes the ambiguity worse, which leads to discomfort for the customer, which can lead them feeling uneasy or uncertain about buying from you.

Here's what happens inside the customer's mind:

You say:	This book is white	which means that	it's easy to read
Customer thinks:	So what?	It looks clean?	Oh. So it doesn't look clean then.

You say:	This book is easy to read	because	it's white
Customer thinks:	Is it?	I need some evidence	Oh yes. So it is.

Practice both formats:

- Feature *which means that* Benefit

- Benefit *because* Feature

13.1   Features and Benefits

Write down ten features of something that a customer might buy from you, and then write down a benefit for each feature.

Feature	Benefit

13.2   Proposals

Whichever medium you use for a proposal, the format is the same:

Problem   The customer's problem or requirement

Cost   What the problem is currently costing the customer

Solution   Your proposed solution

Benefits   The technical and financial benefits of your solution, specific to the customer

Value   The price of your solution

Close   Ask for the customer's business

You might recognise that this sequence mirrors the decision process that the customer has been through.

A written proposal would also include an 'About us' section containing a list of your services and perhaps some examples of customers you have worked with and the problems that you have solved for them.

You can even use this sequence to deliver a verbal proposal to summarise a phone call:

"So let me just check that I understand. You have some new staff who don't have sales experience, which is affecting your sales turnover by around £2000 a month, so you're looking for training which will give you the skills you need to close more business quickly. We can provide that for you for £2000, would you like to go ahead with that and set dates?"

"OK, so to check what I've written down, you are finding it difficult to get parts for your old machine, and that's costing you an extra £500 a month in maintenance services, so if we could supply a new machine to you for £2000 then that would give you reliable service and pay for itself in 4 months. Can I send over a contract for you to look at?"

14: Handling Objections

A customer will raise an objection when you ask for the order and they are not quite ready to make a decision.

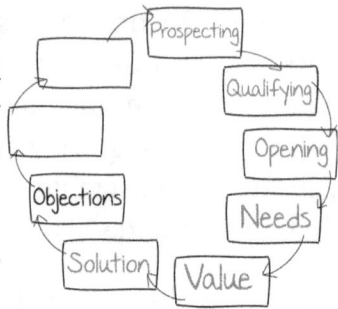

If you've read other sales books or been on training courses, you might expect to see objection handling after closing, because that's when the objections typically arise. As a general rule of thumb, if you get objections, then they are either real, in which case you're closing too early and with insufficient information, or they're fake, in which case you're closing too early and with insufficient information.

We're talking about objections before the closing stage because you can anticipate and deal with most objections before the customer raises them, thereby making it easier to close.

Your customer is likely to raise an objection because:

- They don't want what you're selling badly enough

- The facts of your proposition are unclear

- The needs of the customer are not defined clearly enough

- The benefits of your solution are not matched closely enough to the customer's needs

- Your customer has a concern which, unless resolved, means they will not go ahead

Typically, there are three types of objection:

- True Objections

- Rejections

- Stalls

14.1.1 True Objection

A true objection arises when the customer imagines buying from you, therefore a true objection is a *buying signal*.

A **specific question** relating to a specific piece of information that you have just given your customer is likely to be a true objection.

A **request for more information** on a particular subject shows engagement and is likely to be a true objection.

A point raised to **dispute the accuracy** or validity of your facts is likely to be a true objection. Your customer is seeking factual clarification, rather than blocking you with emotion.

Almost any **specific discussion about money** is likely to be a true objection. Your customer is asking you to make it affordable for them and they wouldn't do this unless they were interested. However, a price objection means that you have not built sufficient value to support your price, and if you wait until you're ready to close, it's often too late to correct because the customer's expectations are already set. If the price objection is non-specific then your customer may be using the 'Mother Hubbard' or a similar rejection to see what they can get away with. Don't under estimate this ruse, I've heard of buyers for a major supermarket using it for an IT services contract worth £14 million. Apparently, as the buyer was about to sign the contract, he said, "Ah, small problem, we don't have £14 million. We have £10 million. Take it or leave it."

14.1.2 Rejection

You may experience a feeling of rejection when:

- There is no logical explanation offered by your customer for their negative behaviour

- There is little substance to your customer's counter argument

- Your customer seems to be working hard at NOT engaging in conversation with you

- Your customer seems interested, then reveals they have no budget

- You feel hurt, frustrated or upset

14.1.3 Stall

Towards the end of the sale, when the customer is being asked to make a decision, they might use stalling tactics to buy themselves time to think.

A customer might stall when:

- They are not motivated enough to buy

- They cannot justify the decision in their own mind

- They are not the decision maker and they have exaggerated their authority

- They think that by pulling back, they will pressure you to drop your price

14.1.4 Negative questions

- How can you justify…?

- What happens if…?

- How does it work when…?

- But…?

- Can't I get that cheaper elsewhere?

- Aren't they unreliable?

The customer's tone of voice is negative and they are essentially saying, "I don't agree with you". However, by asking a question, they are giving you a chance to change their mind. The customer is saying, "This is what I've heard, is it true?"

While the customer may sound negative, remember that they are giving you an opportunity to change their mind. The alternative is that they keep quiet and take their business elsewhere.

14.1.5 Negative statements

We are usually more comfortable with questions than with statements. Questions give us something to answer. Statements make us feel under attack.

When your customer makes a sale threatening statement, turn it into a question that you can answer.

"I don't like the idea of having to change suppliers."

"What is it that concerns you sourcing a better supplier?"

When turning round an objection in this way, the one question to avoid at all costs is "Why?"

"Why?" will get the customer to reinforce their statement, especially if it isn't a true objection.

Instead of thinking, "Why?", think, "How?" or "What if?"

Once again, by raising the objection, the customer tells you that they are engaged in the sales process. The alternative is that they nod politely and then go to your competitors.

14.2 Preventing Objections

- Cover the benefits before the customer has an opportunity to raise the objection

- Focus on the positive rather than the negative

- Sell the customer what they really need and want as opposed to what we *think* they need and want or what they *ask* for

- Be honest about any potential downsides or drawbacks of a solution

- Ask yourself, "Would I buy it?"

14.2.1 How to pre-empt objections

- Before talking to your customer, take a guess at the objections they are likely to raise

- Research solutions to the objection

- Work out the positive interpretation of the situation

- Raise it as a benefit statement before the objection comes up

For example, before your customer says...

"Your company is too small."

You can say... "Because we're small we're able to offer a personal service that you won't get from a large company."

14.3   Handling objections

If you do receive an objection your first response should be neutral support:

- I'm glad you asked me that because...

- I know that's important to you and it's important to me too...

- That's a good point because...

Cost objections can seem difficult to overcome because:

- You know that your competitors could undercut you

- You know what your profit margins are

- You want the business

- If the customer's cupboard is bare, there's nothing you can do about it

But if the customer didn't have any money, they wouldn't be enquiring about your services. We all want the best possible product at the lowest possible price and we all love a bargain, but we also know that you get what you pay for.

In your line of work, a poor quality component could be a life-or-death matter, so if you believe in the quality of what you deliver, don't be afraid to ask a fair price for it.

Dealing effectively with the cost objection is as much about your attitude as it is about your skills. Start by accepting that objecting on the grounds of cost is a fairly natural reaction from someone who does not understand the value to them of what you are offering.

ANY cost is too expensive if there is a lack of perceived value.

When bottled water was first sold in the UK, in the late 1980s, people laughed. Why would you pay for water when it comes free out of your kitchen tap? The drinks companies have slowly created a perception of value in pure, mountain filtered, organic, healthy water to the point that most people will buy bottled water rather than fill a flask from their kitchen tap.

Price objections can arise because:

- The customer wants to 'win' the argument and prove their negotiation skills

- The customer doesn't want to be taken advantage of

- The customer knows from experience that bargaining works in getting prices down

- There is an objection that the customer has not yet raised, so they use cost as a stall

- The customer does not value what you are offering

14.3.1 Handling Price Objections

To find out what's behind a cost objection, ask direct questions such as:

"Are you concerned about the service you will receive?"

Focus your customer on goals and objectives. Get them to remind themselves what they are aiming to achieve, and keep their attention on value rather than price.

"What would be your ideal solution?"

"What's most important in your decision?"

Price is rarely the deciding factor in any sale, because for price to be a decision criteria, the customer must have a choice of identical products. If you want to buy a new camera then you can shop around for the exact same model and choose the cheapest supplier. But with your service, the customer can never make a like-for-like comparison, because features of your service include relationship and expertise which are unique to you.

If you really want to give a discount, position it as a reward for making the right decision, not as an incentive. Always offer a discount with an "If..." statement.

14.4 Common Objections

Plan for the most common objections that you come across.

Objection	Response

15: Closing

We've put closing at the end of the cycle because that's the point at which the customer is ready to place an order and your interaction with them shifts from helping them to make the right decision to actually delivering what they have ordered.

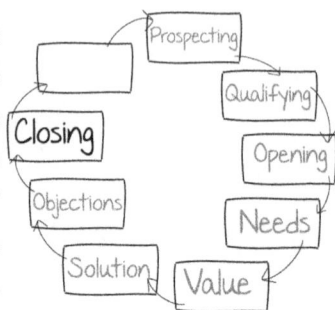

In reality, closing happens at every stage of the sales cycle, because at every stage, some leads are being qualified out and you're focusing more on the ones that you have a better chance of winning.

Any service depends on a consultative sale, because the service is tailored to the needs of the individual customer. Therefore...

In a consultative sales process, the more talking the customer does, the more likely they are to buy.

You will find books and books of closing techniques, here are a few that you will come across.

15.1 Common Closing Methods

15.1.1 Direct – simply ask for the business

- Would you like to go ahead?

- Are you ready to place an order?

15.1.2 Trial – a test for understanding

- How does that look to you?

- How does that sound?

- How do you feel about that?

15.1.3 Alternative – offering a choice

- Do you need us to deliver or will you collect?

- Do you need to set up an account or pay on invoice?

15.1.4 Assumptive – confirming a detail

- When do you need delivery?

- Do you want me to bring some samples over? (Take an order form too!)

Do you actually need closing 'techniques'?

What we could say is that, since the prospect will place an order at the point that the risks balance out on their decision to part with their cash, the prospect will in fact 'close' the deal themselves. When the prospect is at that point, they know that they want to go ahead and buy, but they don't know how to go ahead and buy, because they are not the expert in your ordering processes – you are. So at that point, the prospect needs to know what to do next. Since we all want to predict the future in order to have a sense of security, you can talk your prospect through the ordering process.

"If you want to go ahead, the next step would be for me to take a few details from you, then I'll call you when the carpet is in stock, which normally takes around 3 days, and I'll arrange a time with you for the fitters to come to you, and they'll take no more than 2 hours to fit the carpet."

"If you're ready to go ahead, I'll get a scope of work document over to you and once you've agreed that, we'll arrange dates to make a start."

At every decision point in the process, what the prospect wants is **reassurance**, and when money is about to change hands, they want that more than ever.

15.2 Reinforcing the Decision

Remember to emphasise:

- They have made a good choice

- The process from here on is simple and hassle free

- You are available for any questions they may have

- You appreciate their business

- They will get real benefits from working with you

15.3 Setting Expectations

As soon as you close the sale, the very first thing you need to do is set the customer's expectations by talking them through what will happen next.

Partly, this is about moving them into 'owning mode', and partly it's about reassuring them that they have made the right decision.

Buying a service is inherently risky, because you don't get to find out how good the service is until you've bought it. If things don't work out, you can always ask for a refund, but you've already lost the time that you invested. Many customers stay with poor suppliers in the hope that things will improve rather than go through the pain of finding a new supplier.

While reassurance is important in any decision, in a service sale it is absolutely critical, especially just after the customer makes a buying decision, because they want you to prove that you know what you're doing.

You will achieve this by confidently walking the customer through the post-sale process.

Thank you for your order. What's going to happen now is...

16: Follow Up

One of the most difficult things to get sales people to do is follow up. Many are so grateful to get the customer's order that they daren't go back and ask for feedback in case the customer changes their mind!

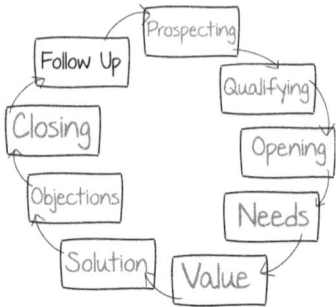

For large orders, it's more common for sales people to ask why they lost.

Hardly any sales people, only the very best ones, will call a customer to ask why they won an order.

Following up serves a number of purposes:

- Learn what you did that worked so that you can do it more often

- Learn what you can improve on

- Reinforce the customer's decision

- Build a long term relationship

- Solicit recommendations and referrals

Questions to ask include:

- Why did you choose to give us your business?

- How would you like me to keep in touch with you?

- Are you happy with the service you received from us?

- What could we have done better?

- Would you be happy to be a reference customer for us?

16.1   Create a Schedule

For each customer, you can create a follow-up schedule to make sure you stay in touch and pick up any future opportunities. If you have calendar software, you could even set up automatic reminders.

After:	Do this:
1 hour	
1 day	
1 week	

1 month	
3 months	
6 months	
1 year	

17: Account Management

When you begin to routinely follow up and keep in touch with your prospects throughout their decision cycle, you have become an Account Manager.

Account management is the set of activities required to build a long term commercial relationship with a customer.

What are the advantages of account management?

Some sales people thinking that visiting a customer on a regular basis for a 'catch up' is account management. Other than the fact that you're talking to an existing customer, your approach should be exactly the same as for dealing with a new business lead; you have to qualify the lead, drive the sales process and help the customer to make the right decision.

You already know the customer's general requirements, but don't allow that familiarity to make you complacent and assume the customer will automatically place an order with you.

Probably the most important feature of account management is that an existing relationship gives you a reason to contact a customer and find out about their future plans. This enables you to influence their decisions and discover opportunities for services that you can provide, but which the customer doesn't know you can provide. This is called 'cross selling'.

When you anticipate a customer's needs before they talk to potential suppliers, you can solve the customer's business problems rather than just responding to their technical requirements. This automatically makes your service more valuable to the client and locks out your competitors. This approach is often called 'solution sales'.

Think back to Jim Holden's 4 level model. Where does an account manager fit within that? Level 4? Not usually. Level 1 is usually not sufficiently focused on the sales target. Levels 2 and 3 are where you'll find most Account Managers, because these are the levels with the target and relationship focus to develop an account relationship.

I'm not going to say a great deal about Account Management because it is quite straightforward, in principle at least. Rather than looking for new prospects through 'cold' lead generation, the Account Manager focuses on prospecting with existing customers. Fundamentally, the Account Manager has to add value to the customer and he or she achieves this by having something to say to the customer other than, "Have you got any orders to place this month?". That's Level 1 order taking, it is not Account Management or even focussed selling.

There are broadly two types of Account Manager.

17.1   Service Account Management

A customer who buys a service from you, such as equipment maintenance, internet access or property management, will have an ongoing need for information about the performance of their service. The Account Manager uses these service conversations to find out about new opportunities and also competitive threats.

The biggest threat to this type of account is the supplier's own complacency, which can create an opening for a competitor to offer better service levels or more attentive Account Management.

17.2 Commodity Account Management

A customer who regularly buys commodities from you such as cleaning products, electrical components or raw materials will have to place regular orders. Rather than simply filling in the order form, the Account Manager uses these conversations to up-sell and cross-sell and also find out about competitive threats.

The biggest threat to this type of account is price, and the Account Manager can counteract this threat by providing added value to the customer, perhaps in the form of education, access to product development teams or joint marketing. The Account Manager might also help the customer with 'emergency' orders, something which the customer might not get from a cheaper supplier where they are just another customer.

17.3 Account Development Plans

Perhaps the most important tool for an account manager is an Account Development Plan, which is simply a way of documenting what you know about a customer and what you plan to do with that knowledge to achieve your commercial goals.

What information should be collected in an ADP?

Current Knowledge:	Business description
	Contacts
	Market analysis
	Customer's competitors
	Account activity to date

Account Potential:	Future plans
	Organic growth
	Cross selling
	Referrals
	Revenue potential
Account Plan:	Short and long term strategy to realise account potential

Create an account plan template that contains the
information you need.

18: Practice

Make notes of new ideas that you have in each of the stages of the sales cycle, and also note your progress and achievements.

Also, create templates for a Needs capture form and an Account Development Plan to record the information that is most relevant for you.

Prospecting

Qualifying

Opening

Needs

Value

Plain Selling

Solution

Objections

Closing

Follow Up

19: Development Plan

Make some developmental goals for yourself which you will be able to measure over time.

Goal	When?	Notes

20: Appendix

4.1 Suggested answers

Type	Who is the customer?	Who is the salesperson?	What's the risk?
Direct	A corporate buyer or procurement manager	A B2B salesperson, either reselling someone else's product or service, or a manufacturer or 'OEM'	Competition, DIY, 'do nothing' Limited sales resources tied up in each sales process
Indirect	Your customer's customer	A manufacturer or 'OEM'	Your customer doesn't represent your product properly to their customer
Channel	A marketing manager or buyer	A manufacturer or 'OEM'	You're reliant on the channel's salespeople
Reseller	A marketing manager or buyer	A manufacturer or 'OEM'	You're reliant on the reseller's salespeople

Retail	The shopper	The person behind the till	Theft, overstock, faulty returns
Wholesale	Wholesale buyer	Manufacturer or importer	No control over sales to user
Outsource	Stake-holders in the end user organisation	A sales team	Contractual delays, ownership of assets, complexity of stakeholder management

21: About Peter Freeth and Genius

Peter Freeth has worked with corporate and SME clients since 2000 to deliver the highest levels of business performance through people development:

- 700% increase in profitability through coaching Parker Hannifin's leadership team

- Enabled the sales director of Logica to deliver £300,000,000 in new business revenue

- £16 Million in lost revenue identified and recovered for Babcock, arising from project mismanagement and poor management controls

- Doubled sales conversion rates for Domestic & General through trainer training

- Doubled sales conversion rates for Fitness Industry Education through sales coaching

- 25% time and cost saving on Somerfield's graduate training program, achieved by identifying and 'blueprinting' the talents of high performers within the business

- 83% success rate for career promotions for 25 'future leaders' through a succession planning program at Babcock

- Coached the sales team of FGI Mercer from 50% of target to all being over target

- Trained 250 of BT's SME sales people in how to get access to a decision maker

- Trained 200 of RSSB's staff in how to engage and influence stakeholders

Peter has written 10 books on various business and leadership subjects as well as countless magazine articles. He has presented at intentional conferences in Poland, Ukraine, Denmark, USA, Canada, South Africa, Turkey, Europe, North Africa, Ireland and the UK and is an expert in the field of developing high performing cultures in business through leadership excellence.

Peter's books are all based on insight and experiences gained from solving real business problems for clients.

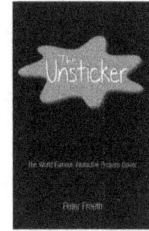

Plain Selling

www.ingramcontent.com/pod-product-compliance
Lightning Source LLC
Chambersburg PA
CBHW022037190326
41520CB00008B/610